From

The Women's Press Ltd
34 Great Sutton Street, London EC1V 0DX

Farida Karodia   *Photo by Gold Photography*

Farida Karodia was born and brought up in South Africa. She taught there for four years and then in Zambia for three before emigrating to Canada. After three years in Canada, she decided to give up teaching so that she could concentrate on her writing.

She wrote several radio dramas for the Canadian Broadcasting Corporation before starting work on *Daughters of the Twilight*, her first novel. She is currently working on her second novel which is also set in South Africa.

FARIDA KARODIA

Daughters of the Twilight

The Women's Press

First published by The Women's Press Limited 1986
A member of the Namara Group
34 Great Sutton Street, London EC1V 0DX

British Library Cataloguing in Publication Data

Karodia, Farida
  Daughters of the twilight.
  I. Title
  823'.54[F]   PS3561.A67/

ISBN 0-7043-5007-6
ISBN 0-7043-4017-8 Pbk

Typeset by AKM Associates (UK) Ltd,
Ajmal House, Hayes Road, Southall, London
Printed by Hazell, Watson & Viney
Aylesbury, Bucks

To Rosemary

One

Sterkstroom is a small dorp in South Africa. It is the type of town that you drive through en route to some other place, happily forgetting that you've ever been there. For us, however, it was home, the only one that my sister, Yasmin, and I had ever known.

There was nothing remarkable about this little town of approximately twenty-five hundred people, not counting the blacks because there were no census figures available for them.

The weather was equally unexceptional – cold in winter and hot in summer, the one difference being that we had an occasional dusting of snow. The high altitude made the summers bearable, except when we had to contend with the berg wind, a hot, suffocating current of air which gusted across the mountains on its way to the ocean. It sapped your energy, stole your breath and whipped up the grey, gritty dust to blast the back of your legs until they stung, leaving your skin prickly with irritation and discomfort.

My grandmother said that the wind brought sickness and death, an observation substantiated by the pealing of funeral bells.

My sister and I had awakened to such a morning on a Sunday several years ago. There had been no point lingering in a bed that was as oppressive as a coffin. Since the coolest spot was the outside bathroom, we both headed for the concrete structure which was protected on one side by the arbour and on the other by the high wall of the cool-room where the produce was stored. Here Yasmin and I dawdled, she in the lavatory and I in the shower, until Papa, wanting in, banged on the door.

Yasmin muttered something about Park Station, but when he knocked again she quickly opened the door and, with a sheepish grin, pushed by him.

We were all a bit irritable, each of us having endured a sleepless night. It wasn't only the heat, but some time in the early hours we had been awakened by the sound of shattering glass. My father had gone out to investigate and had returned with the news that someone had tossed a stone through a store-room window. We knew who the culprit was.

'You'd better speak to the principal about that boy Cobus Steyn,' Papa told a bleary-eyed Ma when she joined us in the kitchen.

'Why don't *you* speak to him, Abdul?' she asked.

But he ignored her and went into the yard to inspect the damage.

Yasmin and I exchanged glances. I knew that she wanted to talk to Ma about the possibility of going to a boarding-school. I waited, expecting that she would say something, but she had obviously noticed the tension and had concluded that this was not the right time.

Yasmin and I hastened outside when Papa returned, uttering a string of curses under his breath.

'I was scared silly when I heard the window breaking,' I confessed. 'What about you?'

'I wasn't scared. I knew it was Cobus Steyn.'

I rolled my eyes in despair. A sound from the gate interrupted. I peered past her shoulder. 'You want to find out what he wants?' I asked, inclining my head to where the *Kwedini* waited.

There never was any rest for us, especially on Sundays or on holidays. The Lord's Day Act shut down all businesses for the sabbath, except ours. On these days we did a steady trade via the back door while the other shopkeepers were singing their hearts out at the Dutch Reformed Church across the street.

On the few occasions when Papa was caught, he pleaded guilty and paid the fine. This rarely happened though, because we were all so careful, particularly my grandmother, Nana, who made sure that the merchandise was well concealed. The youngsters who knew the routine wore loose clothing to hide their purchases. Yasmin was convinced, however, that it was only a matter of time before we all ended up in the Sterkstroom jail.

'Tell him the store's closed,' she grumbled in a voice loud enough for the boy to hear. But he remained, index finger gingerly rubbing the side of his nose, one foot hooked behind his leg, eyes large and watchful.

'Every penny counts,' I reminded her.

'You're beginning to sound like a broken record . . . like Nana,' she remarked drily.

2

'All right, I'll go,' I sighed, braiding my waist-long hair as I walked to the gate.

I had my father's round face, but that's where all resemblance to my parents ended. I accepted without rancour that my sister, with her angular bone structure and large almond eyes, was the beauty in the family. Even my eyelashes were insignificant fringes when compared with hers.

'Don't worry, Meena, some day you'll emerge from your chrysalis,' she had said whenever she found me peering into the mirror. 'Believe me, little sister, you'll unfold just like a butterfly.'

I was grateful to her for this reassurance. It supported me through those insecure days when I became disheartened about my plain face and unremarkable body.

By ten o'clock it was still hot, even though the wind had eased. Papa was in the backyard arranging the bags of potatoes that had to be sent to the Quèenstown market the following day. His lips moved rapidly and I guessed that he was muttering a string of profanities in Gujarati. This was what he usually did when he was angry.

The tension between my parents was increasing. It seemed that neither of them needed much of an excuse these days to argue. Ma was still annoyed with Papa because of his reluctance to deal with Cobus.

I didn't blame her for being upset. Cobus Steyn was rotten to the core. Sitting out there in the shade of the arbour, I remembered the day of my fifth birthday.

Two

I had awakened that morning to find propped up at the foot of my bed a large celluloid doll exactly like the one Lena van Staaden had.

I pushed aside the bedcovers, hitched my drooping pyjama pants and crawled over to where the doll sat with extended arms.

'Come to Mama, Dolly.' I gingerly lifted it. The jointed limbs moved with surprising ease, a feature which compensated for the absence of hair. 'You're my baby now, Dolly,' I cried ecstatically, wrapping my arms about it.

My yelp had awakened Yasmin, who flipped aside her bedcovers and bounced on to my bed. 'Let's show Baboo,' she said, obviously relieved that the strain of keeping the secret was finally over.

'It's like Lena's doll,' I pointed out.

'Ma bought if off Mrs van Staaden,' Yasmin said. 'Come, let's find Baboo.'

Although I had wanted to show the doll to Nana first, I allowed Yasmin to steer me past our grandmother's room to where Baboo was practising his cricket strokes in the backyard.

Baboo was an orphaned second cousin who had come to live with us when I was only two years old. I didn't remember much about his arrival, only that he had been there for as long as I could remember.

Nana said that after his parents had been killed in an accident, he'd been shunted from one relative to another before ending up in Sterkstroom. Ma and Papa took him in regardless of all the warnings about his being a problem.

Cricket was his all-consuming passion, even though there was little opportunity for him to show off his dexterity in Sterkstroom.

Baboo grinned when he saw us. I promptly pushed the doll at him, but he thrust his hands into his trouser pockets. A quick swing in either direction confirmed that this lapse had not been witnessed by any of his pals who might've happened by. He blew out a puff of air and flicked back a dark tendril which had tumbled over his forehead. Before I could get any other ideas, he quickly returned his hands to his trouser pockets while I fixed him with a reproachful glance.

Yasmin, who was only two years older than me, had been trying to get her hands on the doll ever since I discovered it on my bed that morning. When she found me asleep later that afternoon she quietly stole off with it.

According to Yasmin, she was sitting on the curb of the sidewalk outside the house and had failed to notice Jacobus Steyn creeping up behind her.

He reached over her shoulder and plucked the doll from her hands.

'Cobus, please!' Startled, she had leaped up and had managed to grab one of the doll's arms. But she was no match for Cobus. He shoved her. She lost her balance and sat down heavily. Winded, she waited, dark eyes rivetted on him.

'No Cobus, please,' she pleaded. Lunging at him she grabbed hold of the doll's free arm.

'Say Baas Cobus.'

'No!'

'I'm your baas and I can have anything I want.' He jerked and Dolly's arm snapped off in her hands 'Got it!' he sneered, holding her at bay.

'Now see what you've done!' She looked down at the severed arm clutched in her fist, rubber bands dangling grotesquely.

'That'll teach you!'

Yasmin's scream brought me and Baboo running from the backyard. Baboo rounded the corner and spun the Afrikaner youth around. The impetus threw Cobus off balance, and the next moment the two boys were rolling on the ground.

'You filthy bastard,' Baboo grunted through gritted teeth, pummelling the white youth in the stomach.

'You son-of-a-bitch. I'll break your neck,' Cobus hissed, flailing at Baboo's face. Although he was the same age as Baboo, he was a little bigger and heavier. But Baboo's fury had lent him the added strength.

My tortured glance sought that of my sister's. I noticed in a vague, distracted way that she looked a sight. Her hair, loosened from the restraints of the pony-tail, had tumbled to her shoulders.

5

Her new pink organdie dress was streaked with dirt. The white knee socks sagged around her ankles in crinkled folds.

But Yasmin paid no attention to me. She had got right into the spirit of the fight by trying to kick sand into Cobus's face. Unfortunately, Baboo was the one to suffer.

'Hit him, Baboo! Hit him!' she cried, eyes glittering savagely.

Finally Baboo pinned Cobus to the ground and smashed his fist into his face.

I stepped back, shrinking from the sight of blood. But even more devastating was the sight of my mutilated doll, tossed aside, the celluloid dented and fragmented.

Baboo got off Cobus's limp body.

Cobus tasted the blood and blotted his lips with the back of his hand.

Baboo's anger was spent. He dusted his clothes, still keeping a wary eye on Cobus, then he ushered us through the gate.

Once across the street and out of Baboo's range, Cobus recovered some of his bravado. 'I'll get you for this, coolie!'

But this was not the end of the matter. A few weeks later Baboo came home bloodied. Cobus and three friends had laid in wait for him.

Each day brought with it another incident and a new problem. We waited apprehensively.

'Abdul, he's either going to kill or be killed,' Ma predicted.

Papa agreed that something had to be done, so without further delay they dispatched a letter to a relative in Johannesburg. The cousin replied immediately, expressing his eagerness to have Baboo.

Although the decision was a painful one for Ma and Papa, they reasoned that it was for Baboo's own protection. The matter was settled promptly and arrangements were made to send him to his new home.

'It's for his own good,' Papa assured us. 'If he stays, he may get into serious trouble.'

Baboo was reluctant to leave the relative security of his home in Sterkstroom, but he eventually agreed when he was assured that he could play cricket to his heart's content in Johannesburg.

I remember the evening of Baboo's departure so clearly. The whole family had gathered at the station in a solemn little group. His two friends, Moses Dlamini and Willem Arendse, had also come to see him off. They stood by awkwardly, studying the scuffed toes of their shoes while they waited to exchange a few words with him.

Moses Dlamini, the oldest of the three, lived with his mother in the Location, where he attended the African school. Willem Arendse on the other hand lived seventeen miles out of town on Oubaas Nel's farm, where his father was employed as a labourer. Willem and Baboo were both at the Sterkstroom Apostolic Primary School for Coloureds, a one-roomed, whitewashed, concrete building on the town side of the gully, a mere stone's throw from the narrow pedestrian swing-bridge that crossed into the Location.

When the train pulled into the station Ma and Nana were both moist-eyed. They had barely managed to say their goodbyes when the conductor's whistle shrilled and Baboo hurriedly clambered aboard and disappeared inside.

'You look after yourself and be careful,' Ma called. 'Jo'burg is full of tsotsis. Be sure to hide your money, and hang on to your suitcase.'

Baboo reappeared at a window and leaned out. Despite his excitement his eyes glittered with tears when the train jerked forward and slowly slid along the tracks.

We all walked alongside the locomotive to where the platform fell away, waving until the lights dwindled to pin-points and the train was finally swallowed up by the cavernous darkness.

Overcome by a sense of desolation, as if something precious had been torn from us, we remained on the deserted platform listening for the piercing whistle which would indicate the train's arrival at the crossing.

Three

The mention of Cobus Steyn had brought all these memories flooding back. I hadn't given it much thought until that morning under the arbour. I was only thirteen, yet it felt as though this incident with the doll had taken place ages ago, in another lifetime. I watched Papa, who was still stomping about in the backyard, angrily tossing things about.

I hated it when he and Ma quarrelled. There were times when the atmosphere was so fogged with tension that I couldn't sleep. I would lie awake all night listening anxiously to the harsh, angry voices which carried through the thin walls.

Yasmin had a very cavalier attitude towards these incidents, explaining that it was part of the life-cycle, our parents working themselves up into a frenzy only to end up the same old way, making love.

But watching Papa I had my doubts about this. They just seemed so distant, like two strangers. I brooded about the situation, and wondered if it had anything to do with Nana's remark that it was better to be an old man's darling than a young man's slave.

Although the whole concept of love-making was still too complicated for me, I did on occasion find my thoughts wandering in that direction, grappling with the intricacies of adult relationships and, in particular, love-making. I was mortified when these thoughts brought with them a strange fluttering in my thighs and I was left with an uncomfortable moist feeling.

Dora Oliphant had once told me that all women were basically the same and that the only difference was in the size of the opening in older women. This was all due to the fact that these openings stretched for babies to push out, and other things to push in.

The startling sound of squealing tyres scattered the rest of my thoughts. I glanced up in time to see Papa pulling away from the kerb. I assumed that he was driving to Molteno. But in this heat?

In the kitchen Ma confirmed that Papa had gone to Molteno, and with a grimace of relief she tied an apron about her waist. It seemed to me that she was going to cook up a storm despite the tremendous heat.

I loved these occasions. It meant that we women could congregate in the kitchen. With Papa away there was always a feeling of camaraderie amongst us. I think he sensed it, and at times he must have felt left out. But I didn't dwell too much on Papa now. I was thinking more of all the fun we were going to have. There would be lots of gossip and laughter, especially if Yasmin joined in, because she was so good at imitating people.

Gladys, who had anticipated Ma's intentions, had built a huge fire in the stove, and each time the oven door opened we were assaulted by a blast of air hot enough to singe the hair off our legs.

Yasmin joined us and I guessed that she would take advantage of Ma's change of mood. I was right, because before long she gathered her courage.

'Ma, I want to go away,' she said, leaning her hip against the sink.

Ma looked up. She studied Yasmin. Then, becoming aware of the drop of perspiration easing its way down the side of her face, she lifted the corner of her apron and carefully dabbed at her forehead.

Gladys entered, slamming the door behind her. Startled, we all glanced up. Noting Ma's heat-induced irritation, Gladys gave a sheepish grin, her dark cheeks glittering with perspiration. Carrying the freshly shaken mats, she quickly trotted to the front rooms. Her bulky German-print skirt hung from her thick waist and fleshy hips, buffeting her ankles and bare feet. 'Hienie, Khoskhaz, almost finish now.' She straightened her head-dress and waited for Ma's response.

But Ma ignored her. She was too hot, too bothered and too put out by what Yasmin had said. She fixed her attention on the roti dough.

I felt a familiar tug at my insides. I had long ago made the startling discovery that Ma, like Yasmin, had a soft underbelly of vulnerability which was rarely exposed. But I could see it now, and I watched the two faces with a feeling of anxiety.

Ma was shorter than Yasmin, full-busted with a slight waist that curved out to rounded hips. Nana had once told me that Ma was as voluptuous as one of the maidens in Hindu mythology. Papa, being a Moslem, did not appreciate such a comparison.

9

I thought about this word voluptuous and tried to conjure up an image of a Hindu maiden. The only one that came to mind was the picture of the multi-armed goddess, Laxmi, which hung in Mrs Gopal's bedroom in East London. But I'd only seen it a few times and I didn't go anywhere near it after Yasmin told me that the container on the altar beneath the picture held Mr Gopal's ashes.

Only Ma's face wasn't round like that of the goddess in the picture. Her face was angular, with a generous mouth and prominent cheek-bones which framed a captivating pair of eyes. Her still damp, thick, brown hair shimmered and swayed while she moved about.

Setting down her rolling-pin, she turned to Yasmin and said, 'Exactly what are you trying to tell me?'

My glance darted from my mother to my sister. Yasmin glared at me and I promptly feigned disinterest. But I was all ears. Lowering my head I carefully scraped the residue from the pestle and continued the pounding. I was anxious not to miss a word and so the pounding was out of rhythm and I spattered crushed chilli all over the floor. My eyes and nose were running by this time and I had to rush off to find a tissue.

'I've had enough of the stupid Sterkstroom Apostolic Primary School for Coloureds,' Yasmin said as I returned to the kitchen. I wondered how much I had missed.

I waited with baited breath. Nana had said that the school was a dead-end where the girls invariably ended up being sucked into the morass of Location life, sinking into oblivion or growing fat and old with childbearing.

Now, however, when Yasmin expressed her sentiments about the school, Ma's brows gathered in dismay. 'I suppose you'd like to add your penny's worth too?' She unexpectedly turned on me, catching me slack-jawed.

'Don't pick on me, Ma.' I was startled. 'I'm not the one who wants to leave. I'm quite happy here.'

Ma's glance swept to Yasmin and then back to me.

'You're always ready to take your sister's side,' she said.

I maintained a prudent silence.

'Yasmin, in just another year you'll be in standard nine. It would be much easier if you were to start Senior Certificate at a new school. In a year's time things may change and, who knows, we may be able to send you to a city school. Meena's only two years behind you. If you wait a year she can start her standard seven in the city . . .' Nana entered and Ma's voice trailed away.

'What's going on?' Nana asked, hastening to the stove where she lifted the pot-lids.

Ma shook her head, her face dominated by her wide, dark eyes. This habit Nana had of opening the pots infuriated her. It was a sensitive matter, she had complained to Papa, which touched her pride and self-esteem.

The cooking vessels belonged to Nana, brought with her when she moved in, thus giving her certain inalienable rights in the kitchen.

Years of constant use, however, had practically worn the cooking vessels through. The holes had been soldered so often that the large gobs of lead on the bottoms sent the pots careening across the hot surface of the stove. It was marvellous to watch them do their little jig from the side to the centre of the stove, where it was hottest. ·

'Something's burning!' Nana said sharply.

Startled out of my daydreaming I rushed to the stove also. The scent of Nana's eau-de-Cologne was overpowering. Cursing under her breath Ma dragged the pots to the side, away from the heat.

I returned to my chore, sniffing from the pungency of the chillies. My eyes flitted from my mother to my grandmother.

Nana had just come out of the shower. Her long grey hair, knotted into a bun, had dried instantly and was plastered to her head. She looked much younger than her age, which was somewhere in the late sixties or early seventies. No one knew for sure how old Nana was because she refused to say.

Nana, sensing the mood in the kitchen, swivelled her eyes. They were brown and piercing, with the uncanny knack of ferreting out the most carefully guarded secrets. The small hump on the bridge of her nose marked the spot where her reading-glasses rested, and although she was taller than Ma, the resemblance was unmistakable.

Ma and Nana belonged to that nebulous group generally referred to as Coloured. Oupa Byrne had had a background quite similar to Nana's, but it was only after his death, some time before Yasmin's birth, that Nana came to Sterkstroom.

'What's going on?' Nana asked again.

'Yasmin wants to leave school.'

'That's not what I said,' Yasmin groaned.

'Well, what did you say?' Nana inquired.

11

'I said . . . this school . . . here in Sterkstroom . . .' Yasmin said, impatient with Ma because she failed to understand.

But there was no further explanation required. Nana and Ma exchanged knowing looks.

'What do you want to do?' Nana asked, rearranging the pots on the stove.

'I don't know,' Yasmin muttered.

'You're almost grown up now,' Nana remarked. 'Surely you should know. It's time that you take your lumps. If you want to go out into the world, you'd better realise that it's not an easy place, and you can't run back here each time you're in trouble.'

'Mum, we're not chucking her out of the house. All we're doing is considering another school. Perhaps the change will do her good.'

'What do you have in mind?' Nana asked.

I could tell that Nana was vexed by the way Ma had jumped to Yasmin's defence.

'I have to discuss it with Abdul first.'

'I suppose she's already thought of something.' The corners of Nana's mouth dropped disapprovingly.

Ma banged the spoon down on the table and glared at her mother. 'Sometimes I think that in this day and age this whole business of a joint family is an anachronism.'

'What have I done? You're so quick to fly off the handle, man. I just wonder where you'll find a whipping boy when I'm not around anymore,' Nana said in a trembling voice.

'Let's drop it, Mum,' Ma snapped.

'You've got to stop giving in to her like this, man. One of these days you're going to regret it.'

'Let's just forget it, Mum.'

'Ja. That's okay by me,' Nana muttered, satisfied that she had got in the last word.

There was a momentary pause while Nana looked about her. 'Where on earth is Gladys?'

'She's in the front finishing off the bedrooms. I told her she could leave early.' Ma's reply was curt and defensive.

'All this pampering,' Nana snorted. 'I'm the only one who ever does any real work around here. But no one shows me any appreciation. No one shows anything . . .' she declared, giving Yasmin a frosty look. There was a long pause while Nana tried to extricate herself without losing face. 'Well . . .' she mumbled. 'The

Jo'burg train is due any minute. I'm going to the station to pick up the Sunday paper.'

'I'll come with you, Nana,' I said. I finished what I was doing, got up and stood in the doorway. My glance travelled from my sister, who was sullenly staring at her shoes, to my mother, who was furiously ladling ghee into a pan.

Four

The station was located at the southern end. Our house was on the main street opposite the Dutch Reformed Church. The gravel road to the left veered north-west to Molteno, thirty miles away, and the one to the right snaked around the town for seven miles before it linked with the main Johannesburg–East London Route.

All the streets were unpaved. When traffic was heavy, windows and doors had to be shut to keep out the dust. Wind too was an aggravation, blowing the fine, black coal-dust off the abandoned mounds to cover everything with a grey sheen. It was worse when there was a hot berg wind, like today. Whenever we complained about these conditions, Nana reminded us that it was the mine which kept Sterkstroom alive.

Three blocks south of our house on Church Street a small park formed the town square. The white-owned stores, the two banks, post office and hotel were located here.

It was quite usual for the farming community to gather at the homes of friends and relatives following worship on Sundays. Although the streets were busy now, by evening they would again be deserted.

Nana and I walked in silence, our curious glances flitting from one side of the street to the other.

'By tomorrow morning all those suits will be back in mothballs,' Nana observed when we passed a group of Afrikaner men who were huddled in conversation.

'Hello Nana,' Mrs DuPlessis called from her gate.

'Hello Mrs DuPlessis,' Nana said distantly, obviously resenting the familiarity of the other woman's greeting. Familiarity bred contempt, Nana often said, adding that it was best to keep one's distance with *these people*. She raised her eyebrow a fraction to convey this sentiment.

14

Mrs DuPlessis was one of those Afrikaners helped by Mohammed's General Store through all the rough times when they were denied credit at the white stores. But the moment their circumstances improved, she and the rest of the poor white community all trooped back to their own kind.

'Hoe gaan dit vandag?' Mrs DuPlessis inquired.

Nana nodded and took a deep breath while Mrs DuPlessis leaned against the gate.

I drew in my breath, expecting a long litany of complaints, but to my surprise Nana was brief.

'I can't complain about my health. I'm just grateful when I can get up in the morning and put on my shoes,' she said.

I watched as Mrs DuPlessis, robbed of an appropriate response, cast her eyes around for a distraction. It came in the form of fat Mrs Prinsloo, who waddled by leaning on the arm of Tickey, the slight African girl who usually escorted her to church. In her free hand Mrs Prinsloo clutched her leatherbound Bible.

Mrs DuPlessis smiled at the panting woman while we seized the opportunity to escape.

'Hello Mrs Prinsloo,' Mrs DuPlessis gushed as we moved away. I tried for the sake of propriety to keep my eyes averted from the elephantine rolls of fat which engulfed Mrs Prinsloo. The two women were so engrossed in conversation that neither had noticed our departure.

'I wonder how Piet Prinsloo puts up with her,' Nana muttered.

I, however, had turned to stare thoughtfully after Mrs Prinsloo's maid, Tickey, who would be allowed only to the church gate. Once there one of the Afrikaner sisters from the congregation would be on hand to assist Mrs Prinsloo into the all-white domain.

'What if I end up like Tickey, working for some stupid white woman?' Yasmin had asked one afternoon after Tickey had been in to do Mrs Prinsloo's shopping. The mere thought of such a possibility had sent a shudder of revulsion through my sister. For the first time I was beginning to get some inkling of what went on in Yasmin's mind, and the extent of her dread at being trapped in Sterkstroom.

The vacant lot beside the station was densely treed. A brown carpet of needles crunched underfoot as we hurried along the winding path. The heady scent of pine blended with the aromatic eucalyptus from the clump of trees at the far end.

A train whistle shrilled, sending a startled flock of finches into

15

the sky. The crash of jolting carriages and the hiss of steam heralded the departure of the Jo'burg special. Nana and I hastened into the small café.

Five

'Your Papa is back,' Nana said.

'It's about time,' Ma said, peering through the window when we heard the old DeSoto grinding to a halt.

Papa looked exhausted. Ma stared after him and I suspected that she felt a pang of guilt about their earlier disagreement.

'Go see if your Papa needs anything,' she quietly instructed me.

But before I could get out of my chair Yasmin had leaped up and rushed after him. I followed behind them and stood in the doorway to the bedroom.

Yasmin fussed like a mother hen while he removed his khaki dust-jacket and threw it over the back of the blue padded chair. Then he rolled back his sleeves and slipped out of his braces. Without saying a word, she lifted the porcelain jug of water over his cupped hands and poured. After splashing his face with cold water he emptied the porcelain basin with its pattern of blue forget-me-nots and carefully placed it back on the washstand.

Papa was sixty-five, but tonight he looked even older than Nana. There was a strange look on Yasmin's face, as though she was seeing for the first time that he had aged. In my eyes too he had suddenly become an old man, balding and stooped, his brown arms covered with matted grey hair. My heart skipped a beat as Yasmin gave me a despondent look.

'Are you all right, Papa?' she asked. She was tall like him, with Ma's eyes, but with his long, lustrous lashes. Nana had often remarked about how this feature was wasted on a man.

'We can eat whenever you're ready!' Ma called from the kitchen.

He patted Yasmin's cheek and she gave him an affectionate smile, but there was still a sad look on her face, and I felt a chill. I shuddered, goose bumps springing up on my arms.

'Let's eat,' Papa said, slipping his arms through the braces, which snapped back into place over his shoulders.

17

I walked ahead. Yasmin followed us to the dining-room, where Papa drew the old wicker armchair up to the table and waited for the women to serve the meal.

Yasmin sat down beside him. 'I'll keep you company, Papa,' she offered.

I scowled at her and went into the kitchen to help Ma carry in the dishes of food.

Papa smiled contentedly, peering at Yasmin from beneath his bushy brows. 'What's the matter?' he asked. Although he had an excellent command of both English and Afrikaans, he spoke with a slight accent which identified his Indian origins.

'She wants to leave school,' I blurted out, before Yasmin could say anything.

'Is this true?' Papa rested his surprised glance on her.

Yasmin narrowed her eyes at me. 'Yes, Papa.'

'Why?' he asked. 'There's nothing wrong with this school. That woman is no longer here. Miss . . . Miss . . . What was her name? That teacher?' he asked, looking around for someone to supply the name.

I obliged again. 'Miss Durant.'

The mention of Miss Durant elicited varying reactions from us. We all recalled too vividly the incident with the readers.

It was my first day at school and I was thrilled. But Yasmin, who had already been attending school for two years, regarded it as a bore. She sat on the steps of the one-roomed school house, knees supporting her elbows, face propped on her hands in an attitude of total dejection.

I was glancing around the school yard looking for familiar faces when Willem Arendse came into view, sweat dripping. Summer and winter, dry and rainy season, Willem ran the seventeen miles to school. He had the easy lope of a long distance runner and Yasmin said the principal had high hopes for him.

Disgruntled, she had once remarked that she could never have his dedication for an education. As the sweat-drenched Willem joined his friends, I was inclined to share my sister's opinion.

Most of the Coloured students were from the Location; others, like Willem, came from the surrounding farms. During the lambing and shearing season the attendance dropped dramatically, resuming normal levels when all the work was done.

I had joined the beginners, who were bunched together, voices pitched with shrill excitement, while we awaited the morning bell.

It rang five minutes later and we bumped and jostled before organising ourselves into four uneven lines.

Inside, the junior classes were separated from the seniors by a faded, red, velvet curtain. Since the only exit was through the front of the building, the senior boys who wished to leave the room, in order to attend to the calls of nature or nicotine, had to traipse through Miss Durant's classroom.

Yasmin sat right up at the front of the class in the first desk to Miss Durant's right, sandwiched in between Sarah Schoeman, Anna Klassen and the hefty Dora Oliphant.

While we settled in, Miss Durant carefully cleaned her reading-glasses. Before directing her comments at the older students, she swept a disdainful glance over the newcomers. Satisfied that the young ones were suitably intimidated, Miss Durant perched her glasses on her nose and opened her small notebook.

She ordered us to our feet and, before reciting the Lord's Prayer, we sang out 'Good morning, Miss Durant.' While she completed the registration, we were left to our own devices. Although the class was perfectly silent and attentive, she intermittently rapped the desk with her ruler.

Miss Durant first addressed herself to the right where the older children were seated. She crossed her legs and rested her elbows on the table. Then, supporting her chin on her clasped hands, she surveyed the group as a whole.

'I see many of our old friends are back with us, some of them having advanced a year, others unfortunately . . .' and here her tone became condescending, 'are still in the same old class.'

Her mood recovered, embracing those students who had moved ahead. 'For those of you who have passed into higher classes, remember, I shall be expecting great things from you this year.' At this point she turned her attention to the newcomers. 'I wish to welcome all the new children to SAPS for Coloureds.' She paused. 'I suppose you all know what the letters SAPS stand for?'

A few hands shot up.

She singled out one of the boys who was flapping both his arms in the air.

'Sterkstroom Apostolic Primary School,' he yelled.

I was spellbound, but Yasmin merely rolled her eyes. And while Miss Durant's voice droned on monotonously she became heavy-lidded.

'Now, little ones, if I can have your attention for a moment.'

19

Miss Durant rapped the desk again. The startled Yasmin jumped and Miss Durant glared. 'We have finally received our supply of readers,' she announced, pointing to a pile of *Dick and Jane* readers stacked in the corner of the room.

We all craned our necks to get a glimpse of the precious books. Without them the teachers had been forced to improvise with flashcards and other simple reading material, she explained.

'We're very fortunate to get these readers,' she continued. 'Meneer Bezuidenhout, the superintendent, brought them down here for our very own use, so we must promise to take extra good care of them.'

On the inside covers the books were marked with the oval stamp of the Sterkstroom Primary School for Whites. The books were outdated by about twenty years. This was obvious from the style of dress. Some of the pages were so badly defaced that they left great gaps in the story about the pretty white girl named Jane who had two adoring parents and a dog named Rover.

We eagerly studied pictures of Jane and Rover, Jane and her mother in their kitchen, Jane standing by the picket fence waving at her father, who, briefcase in hand, ambled up the pathway to the house. There were the usual giggles which followed obscene comments about Jane's activities, but Miss Durant quickly brought this silliness under control with several sharp raps on her desk.

I did not participate in this frivolity. Yasmin and I had both learned to read at an early age and now, turning the pages, I concentrated on the captions beneath the pictures.

I was oblivious to everything around me and did not see Yasmin trying to get my attention. I noticed her for the first time beside my desk just as I was about to turn the flyleaf. There, to my horror, beneath the oval stamp on the inside cover were the carefully printed words of a jingle: 'Coolie, coolie, ring the bell; coolie, coolie, go to hell.'

Without a second thought, I ripped out the offensive page.

It drifted to the floor, like a leaf shed from a tree, and fell beside my foot. The tense silence caught my attention and I looked up into the enraged face of the teacher.

'How dare you!' Miss Durant croaked. 'How dare you!' she cried again, almost choking on her words.

My foot slowly edged forward towards the page. But it was too late.

'I'm going to give you the lashing of your life,' Miss Durant cried, yanking me to the front of the class.

'It's only a blank page, Miss Durant,' Yasmin squeaked. Our petrified glances fixed on the cane, which swished back and forth, catching in the folds of Miss Durant's skirt as it swooped downwards in a tight arc.

'Hold out your hand,' she commanded. But at that moment I was incapable of moving.

'You can't cane her!' Yasmin finally found her voice.

'What was that!' Miss Durant's incredulous glance slid off me, sweeping to the source of this defiance.

'She's only a baby . . .' Yasmin mumbled into her shirt collar, her eyes fixed on her shoes.

'Well, if that's the case, you can come forward and take her punishment.'

A dark flush spread over Yasmin's face. She licked her dry lips, considering her options. Her glance lowered, momentarily becoming trapped between the cracks in the floorboards. Then it slowly swept up the wall, lingering on a stain before sliding sideways to the teacher's face.

Miss Durant fixed her mouth into a hard line. 'Give me your hand.'

Yasmin hesitated. She had obviously not counted on this.

'Now girl! Give me your hand!'

Yasmin held out her hand. But she withdrew it the moment the cane swept downwards.

'If you do that again,' Miss Durant said through clenched teeth, 'you'll be in a lot more trouble.'

My eyes followed the upward arc of the cane and I anticipated the searing pain. Yasmin squeezed her eyes shut. When the cane landed, it was like an explosion, and I could almost feel it biting through her flesh to the very bone. I felt the pain speeding up my arm, just as it must have gone up hers.

Before she could recover from the first lash, the second scorched along the same path. I bit into my lower lip to prevent the cry which had gathered in my throat.

Incensed by this defiance, Miss Durant gave her two more lashes for good measure.

Yasmin returned to her seat. She had not uttered a single cry or shed a single tear. The only audible sound was my sobbing.

21

Yasmin's eyes clouded over. The mention of Miss Durant's name had brought its own pain for her. But she tossed her head, showing her reluctance to dwell on these unpleasant recollections.

I couldn't blame her for this. Miss Durant had caused her enough distress.

Yasmin reached for the salt and glared at me. 'Who cares about Miss Durant? I've forgotten all about her. All I know is that Sterkstroom is a dull, boring pimple on the earth's surface. I bet no one outside this place has ever heard of it.'

'It's more like a valley where all the old elephants come to die.' Papa felt obliged to restore to Sterkstroom the dignity that Yasmin had stripped by her remark.

Ma dragged her chair to the table while Nana joined us, and after muttering the blessing, *Bismillah*, all hands descended on the dahl and roti.

'It's a good little school.' Papa was anxious to keep the family intact. 'Miss Durant was no good and we were glad to get rid of her, but you have good teachers now,' he continued.

'Papa, you're all being old-fashioned,' Yasmin said. 'Those two teachers are numbskulls.'

'Where did you learn to speak of your teachers with such disrespect?' Ma was aghast.

But Yasmin didn't care. 'Well, it's true.'

Papa listened, agitated by this exchange.

I watched the shadows creeping up behind Yasmin's eyes.

'What are we going to do about the broken window, Papa?' she asked, backing off.

'The next time I'm in Queenstown I'll buy a piece of glass and maybe Daniel can fix it. In the meantime we'll cover the hole with cardboard.'

'Something's got to be done about that boy, man,' Nana said.

'Why don't we drive out to their farm? Maybe next Sunday,' Papa said.

'It won't do you any good.' Nana reached for another roti.

'Why not?' he asked.

'Because I've already written notes to both the principal and his father.' A wisp of hair had come undone, falling over Ma's ear. Her right hand carried the food to her mouth while the left hand reached over to sweep the strands back under the knot. 'The last time was when he threw stones on the roof.'

There was a moment of silence, for they all recalled vividly the terrifying sound of stones clattering on corrugated iron.

'Steyn is a big shot. He's an MP,' Nana reminded them.

'Big shot or not, he'll have to do something about his son,' Papa said, irritated by his mother-in-law's persistence.

'There must be something wrong with him. Wouldn't he be about eighteen now, the same age as Baboo?' Nana asked. 'Maybe he's retarded.' She rambled on for some moments before realising that Papa was glaring at her. She fell silent, tugging at her collar. There was a tenseness in the atmosphere which only served to remind her that she was living under someone else's roof.

At times, however, Nana seemed to ignore the tension and forge ahead, often recklessly, secure in her belief that she was indispensable.

'Did Delia not summon me to help with you children? Did I not give up everything to respond to this call for help?' she often asked me. On a few occasions during their heated arguments Ma had denied this. The truth, Ma claimed, was that she had taken pity on Nana, because she was living alone. I didn't know whom to believe; all I knew was that despite Nana's grumbling she thoroughly enjoyed our occasional dependence on her.

'What happened about the car?' Ma asked, getting up to refill the dish with dahl.

'Well,' Papa hesitated. 'Mr Swanepoel thinks it needs more work.'

'Expensive work?' she asked, returning to the dining-room.

'No. I can get Jannie to do it.'

'People can't pay. You're wasting time and money with all the tinkering Jannie has to do.' Ma's tone was edged with impatience.

Yasmin and I exchanged glances. It seemed that there was another storm looming on the horizon.

'We haven't done too badly, in spite of the fact that everyone thinks this is a dying town,' Papa observed. 'Have *we* not always had food on our table and a roof over our heads?'

'That's true,' Nana agreed.

'Things will improve.' Papa spoke as though he needed to convince himself. 'We'll live quite comfortably when I sell a few cars.' His voice was wistful and my heart went out to him.

'Stop dreaming,' Ma snapped.

'Do we have to talk about this at supper?' Yasmin groaned

'One car sale is equivalent to a year's produce sales,' he said, ignoring Yasmin and giving Ma a significant look.

'The last time you sold a car the fifty rands profit was swallowed up in HP costs, legal fees and those two retread tyres we had to throw in as part of the deal.'

'Someone up there is taking care of us, man. I can't see how else we've managed,' Nana sighed, rolling her eyes heavenwards.

Papa had had about all he could take of this conversation. 'Things are bound to get better,' he said. 'The boom will come and when it does, I'll be right there to take advantage of it.' He pushed his chair back and went into the kitchen to wash his hands.

He had come from India in search of adventure. At the age of fifteen he arrived in Durban with other Indian immigrants who had come to South Africa as indentured labourers to work the sugar plantations in Natal. He had arrived in the period following the turmoil created by Mahatma Gandhi's call for civil disobedience, a time when the provinces of Natal and Transvaal had passed laws restricting the movement of Indians from one area to another. All East Indians over the age of eight were required to register. They were fingerprinted and issued with identity cards which had to be presented on demand.

But Papa, like thousands of other Indians, had managed to slip through the borders and had escaped to Dordrecht, where he had married his first wife.

There were no children from this marriage and after her death he moved to Aliwal North, where he had met and married Ma, who was twenty-five years younger than he. Shortly afterwards they had settled in Sterkstroom.

After supper Yasmin and I helped with the dishes. When everything had been cleared in the kitchen, Yasmin sat before the stove, raking the coals. Then she watched, half-mesmerised, as the bright embers plopped into the pan of grey ash beneath the grate.

Nana gathered her knitting and shuffled off to her room in the backyard, a single room which had been especially built for her. There were times when Nana resented the way her position was defined.

'But what can you do when you're dependant on a daughter and a son-in-law?' she asked. 'It's okay for now, because I'm still of some use, but where do you go when you have outlived your usefulness?'

Six

The following Sunday Ma and Papa made plans to drive to Hermanus Steyn's farm. I went along for the ride.

'Twee Jonge Gezellen' lay fifteen miles north of Sterkstroom on the leeward side of Penhoek mountain. As far as the eye could see, the green of well-irrigated pastureland graced the foot of the mountain. Ma stopped the car for a moment and listened. The only sound breaking the silence was the creak of the windmills, fanned by a gentle breeze.

Beside the windmills the rippled surface of a large dam gleamed in the midday sun. Beyond this the landscape was dotted with clusters of cream-coloured bundles which looked like rocks but which, on closer inspection, turned out to be sheep.

At the entrance to the farm we bumped off the tar road on to a gravel track and stopped beneath a board on which the name 'Twee Jonge Gezellen' was carved.

I got out to open the gate and Ma drove through. Two miles and six gates later we topped the last hill.

Tucked into the valley was a gabled house, blindingly white like a patch of freshly fallen snow against the green and ecru of the landscape. We passed through the gate and Ma slowed down for the dogs which were chasing after the car, teeth bared, viciously snapping at the moving tyres.

Fortunately, a male servant who witnessed our plight came over and with a series of short whistles brought the dogs under control.

Papa waited until the dogs had slunk back to their pens before he ventured out of the car. 'Steyn, where is he?' he asked, speaking to the tall Xhosa in his own dialect.

The man gestured towards the house. I climbed out and went after Papa. We had just started in the direction of the house when Hermanus Steyn emerged.

He seemed to be fiftyish. He was tall and lean, his muscular chest

25

daringly revealed by the three buttons on his shirt that were left undone.

Papa stood to one side, waiting for Hermanus to invite us on to the stoep, where several chairs were grouped on either side of the door beneath two long, shuttered windows.

Steyn studied Papa closely from under his hat, which was tilted forward hiding his eyes. He idly scratched the side of his neck and waited, a small contemptuous smile playing round the corners of his lips. 'Mohammed! What do you want?' he growled in Afrikaans.

'It's about your boy,' Papa responded in English.

'What about him?'

It was obvious that he was not going to speak English and Papa was determined not to speak Afrikaans. They continued, like two parallel tracks, running in the same direction.

Hermanus stepped forward. He blocked the doorway, thoughtfully tapping a thin leather sjambok against the side of his leg. 'Well . . . speak up. What has my son done to bring you all the way out here?'

'He broke one of my windows.'

For a moment Hermanus looked at Papa, his expression incredulous. Then he laughed, a great roar which seemed to drift over the hills in waves of insolence. At a loss, Papa rested his perplexed glance on me. I could tell that he thought Steyn was quite mad.

'You came all this way to tell me about a piece of broken glass!' Steyn gasped, finally managing to catch his breath.

Papa was embarrassed. Even I felt a little awkward about coming out to the farm to report something as frivolous as a pane in a window. But then Papa remembered that the glass was not the issue. It was the disdain Cobus showed for our property.

Papa was standing at ground level with Steyn on the stoep four feet above him almost dwarfing him. Papa stepped back.

'Come up here,' Steyn said, beckoning Papa to join him.

'Do you understand . . .' Papa began.

'No,' Hermanus silenced him. 'I do not understand why anyone would waste their time like this.'

Papa shook his head. 'It is not the piece of glass, but all the trouble your boy has caused us.'

Steyn studied him. Then abruptly his mood became conciliatory. 'Look, I know that in the past the boy was wild. I was not able to do much with him after his mother died, but they did straighten him out at boarding-school.' He fingered his chin. 'Seems to me some time ago I had a note from one of you that he had thrown stones on your roof.'

'My wife wrote that letter.'

'If it is a new window you want . . . I will pay for it.'

Papa shook his head; he was wasting his time. He got up to leave. 'If I ever catch him interfering with my family . . .'

Hermanus Steyn slowly drew himself erect. 'If you harm my boy, I will have your hide.'

Papa winced, drawing his shoulders forward to shield himself from the Afrikaner's insulting manner.

'You remember your place or one of these days you will end up in the bush, where you belong.' His voice was low, his blue eyes cold and contemptous.

A small vein throbbed at the side of Papa's head. He glanced away, embarrassed that I had witnessed his humiliation.

Ma, sensing the tension, came over to the stoep. Papa had his back to her.

Papa said, 'My name is Abdul and you may be a big man amongst your people, but you're not big enough to have my hide.'

Hermanus Steyn, however, had not heard a word. His attention was fixed on Ma.

Papa turned and saw Ma. 'I am ready to leave,' he said.

Hermanus' frank and admiring gaze elicited a dark flush which crept upwards from Ma's neck. For a brief moment her glance locked with his. The look he gave her was unmistakable, and for a fraction of an instant her lips compressed into a thin, scornful line. Then her glance swept away, dismissing him.

'Mevrou,' Hermanus said, speaking directly to her. 'I will have your window replaced, and I regret my son's bad behaviour.' His English was heavily accented, but flawless.

Papa was astonished at the change in Steyn.

Ma nodded, then turned. Grasping me by the shoulder, she propelled me towards the car. She and I both turned to glance back. Hermanus Steyn was still staring after us.

Seven

Nana was in the shop when Hermanus Steyn arrived the following Tuesday afternoon accompanied by his carpenter, Boesak.

He seemed relieved that Papa wasn't home. When Nana saw him she became quite agitated. I still didn't like him, even when he smiled at me and casually inquired after Ma, who was in the backyard pruning the honeysuckle bush.

Nana had that tight-lipped look which made me suspect that something was up. I remembered now too the way Hermanus had stared after us on Sunday when we left 'Twee Jonge Gezellen'.

I watched as he strolled into the backyard in search of Ma. Nana moved over to the window which overlooked the yard. Curious to see what was going on, I joined her.

Ma didn't seem at all surprised to see him.

'Good day, Mevrou,' he said.

'Good day, Mr Steyn.'

They were standing just beyond the window and we had a clear view of them. I felt an uneasy tug as I watched Ma's hand creeping to her hair, smoothing it back selfconsciously.

Hermanus also noticed the fluttering hand, suspended and trembling like the wings of a butterfly. He smiled boldly. 'I could not rest until I saw you again.'

'I don't think your coming here is such a good idea,' Ma said.

When Hermanus looked up and saw us at the window, the smile left his face, but he feigned indifference.

'Why not?' he asked, brows arched, ignoring her icy tone. He smiled indulgently, and the way he looked at her seemed to say that he knew all about women and their indecision.

Ma looked up and saw us at the window. She became flustered and didn't quite know whether to walk away or to stay and talk to him. In the meantime Boesak stood to one side waiting. Nana was grunting beside me, her eyes narrow slits.

'My husband isn't home,' Ma said loudly.

'Ja, I know. I am not here to see him. I am here to fix your window.'

Ma was selfconscious. It was a quality that seemed to appeal to him. He smiled again.

'Well, what do you think of 'Twee Jonge Gezellen'?' he asked.

Nana gritted her teeth and nudged me with a bony elbow.

'Frankly, I didn't expect to find an old Dutch home right here in our district.'

'It is not an original,' he laughed. 'You only find this type of architecture in the Western Cape, where the big wine farms are. My late wife, rest her soul, liked the simple style so much that we had it duplicated by a very clever fellow.'

'I read somewhere that they're restoring many of those old homes in the Cape.'

He shrugged disinterestedly. 'I do not care one way or another. To me a house is a house.'

In the exchange they had forgotten that old Boesak was waiting. He coughed discreetly.

'Where is the window?' Hermanus asked brusquely.

'In the back.' Ma gestured towards the yard.

'Gaan aan met jou werk.' Hermanus instructed Boesak to get on with his work, then returned his attention to Ma. 'I would be very happy to show you the rest of the house. Would Sunday be convenient?'

They had moved away from the window. I didn't like the way he was smiling at my mother. There was something sinister about him, something that chilled me.

'No, thank you.'

A tell-tale flush spread over Ma's face.

They were now in behind the store-room and Nana and I moved to the other window. Ma saw us and distanced herself from Hermanus by moving off to watch Boesak, who was removing shards of glass from the damaged pane.

'Well, it is up to you; the invitation is open,' he said, following her.

'If you'll excuse me, I have a great deal to do,' Ma said.

I wished he would go. I didn't like him and my heart was pounding with anxiety. The faint scent of Ma's perfume, Evening in Paris, still lingered in the store-room. What were they saying? He

29

was standing so close to her that with the slightest movement he might easily have touched her.

Hermanus studied Ma from under lowered lids. Nana glared.

'I shall look forward to seeing you soon,' he said in a low voice, but not low enough for us.

Ma lifted her head and, with as much dignity as she could muster, said, 'Good day, Mr Steyn.'

By the time she entered the store her nostrils were flared and her chin quivering.

'What's the matter with you?' Nana asked.

Instead of directing her anger at Hermanus Steyn, Nana got the brunt of it. 'That was an unforgivable thing for you to do.'

'What are you talking about?' Nana asked in round-eyed innocence.

'You know very well what I'm talking about.'

Nana shrugged.

'You were spying on me!'

'You're out of your mind,' Nana said scornfully.

'Oh, I know you well enough.'

'Isn't that just like you. Why didn't you tell him to bugger off? Instead you were smiling, simpering like a schoolgirl. You've been acting up lately. Is Abdul not good enough for you any more?'

'Don't be ridiculous!' Then, throwing her hands up in despair, Ma cried, 'There's no use arguing with you!'

Nana sniffed, turned her back on Ma and stalked out of the store-room just as Yasmin entered. She sensed the strain and raised a questioning eyebrow, but I hurried out after Nana.

When Papa returned he was surprised to find that Hermanus Steyn had kept his word and had actually fixed the window.

'Good thing you went to see him, Papa. It looks like he's done a good job,' Yasmin remarked, running her fingers over the smooth surface of the putty.

'I could do a good job like that too, if I had his tools,' Daniel said, taking exception to this remark.

Yasmin saw the hurt look in his eyes and she smiled. She and Daniel got along well. Although she teased him a lot she seemed to enjoy his eccentricity.

After five years he was still an enigma. He had shown up at the gate one day, jacket hanging from bony shoulders, trousers threadbare. In spite of his appearance, there was a strange air of dignity about him that touched us all. Because he couldn't speak a word of Xhosa or Afrikaans, we assumed that he had come from some distant place. Nana speculated that he might have come from one of the Rhodesias, for he spoke about the 'Water that Thundered'.

We explained his strange behaviour away by tapping our heads and turning our eyes skywards. But not so Papa. Daniel was his crony, a confidant, an accomplice in a house dominated by women.

It seemed that Ma knew from the moment he showed up at our gate that he would be there to stay. As an alien without papers he was not permitted to live in the Location, and since Africans were not permitted in town, he moved with a minimum of fuss into the backyard, where he assumed a crab-like existence beneath the rusted skeleton of the Hudson. Much as Ma wished to see the yard cleaned up, it was going to be virtually impossible to find a new home for Daniel.

Eight

The problem of Yasmin's schooling surfaced again months later. We watched with a sense of helpless resignation as she became increasingly morose, often bursting into tears at the slightest provocation.

She had the ability to cry at will, a technique she said that actors often employed. 'All you have to do is concentrate on something terribly sad, like the death of someone close to you.'

'I thought actors used onion juice,' I said, surprised to learn that there were other methods.

'Not real professionals.'

I sighed. There was so much that I didn't know. Compared to me with my meagre knowledge, Yasmin seemed to possess a limitless store of information. Nana had once remarked that Yasmin inhabited a world quite separate from ours. I suspected that it was Yasmin's way of escaping an environment she found so completely inhibiting.

Our parents' lack of concern about finding her an alternative school incensed Yasmin. 'All they ever do is talk,' she complained.

Then at supper one night while she was listlessly picking through the food on her plate, Papa asked: 'What is wrong, Yasmin?'

Yasmin lowered her lashes, squeezing out the tears. I watched fascinated as two large drops trailed down her cheeks.

'I wish I were dead!' With that she leaped up and ran to the bedroom, slamming the door behind her.

There was a moment's silence. Ma sighed. 'I've made inquiries about the private school for girls near East London. Perhaps we should make an appointment with the headmistress.'

Papa thought about this suggestion. He was reluctant to send Yasmin away from the protection of our home. There were too many pitfalls awaiting a young girl like her. Then of course there was the equally important consideration of whether such a school would provide halal food, food prepared in terms prescribed by ritualistic Moslem laws. 'I think she'll be much better off here in Sterkstroom,' he remarked.

'What happens when she has to go to high school?' Ma asked.

'Why would she want to go to high school? One of these days she'll be married.'

'What if she isn't?'

'She will. She will.' Papa spoke with great conviction.

'What are you up to?' Ma demanded.

'Nothing.'

'Have you been trying to find a husband for her?' she asked.

But Papa would say no more.

Tension in our family was increasing again and I took to spending a great deal of time by myself. But one Sunday when both Ma and Yasmin were out I accompanied Nana to the station for the newspaper.

It was a warm autumn afternoon. The setting sun hovered above the horizon, shading the clouds in various hues of crimson which gave the illusion of a protracted twilight.

'The ash from that volcanic eruption in Hawaii is creating these spectacular sunsets,' Nana explained.

'I'd like to be in a spaceship to see all of this from up there.'

Nana shrugged. 'Man, I just wish they'd stop tampering with things that should best be left alone.'

A goods train pulled out of the station, slowly chugging north along the tracks which skirted town. We walked in silence, Nana casting a reflective glance around the town. 'Getting ahead here,' she observed, 'makes me think of King Sisyphus. I don't suppose you've heard of him?'

I shook my head. I'd heard of King Solomon, but not this other king.

'He was condemned to roll a rock up a hill . . . What in blazes . . .' Nana exclaimed, stopping short. 'Isn't that Yasmin? Why is she dallying in the park?'

Not too far from Yasmin sat Cobus Steyn.

Nana hurried over. When Yasmin saw her she jumped.

'What are you doing here?' Nana demanded.

'Sitting,' Yasmin said. Having recovered from the initial shock,

33

she had managed to slide to the far end of the bench, putting distance between herself and Cobus.

Nana, however, had seen the way she was flicking her eyelashes. 'You're cheapening yourself.'

'I wasn't doing anything . . .' Yasmin retorted, but she shut up, pursed her lips into a delicate little bud and lowered her lashes.

'You'd better watch out, my girl, or you'll be spending the rest of your life behind bars. Are you forgetting that he's white?' Nana asked in a low voice, glancing at Cobus, who sat with his arms stretched along the back of the bench. 'You'd better get home now, young lady.'

Yasmin sauntered ahead and, with an over-the-shoulder glance at Cobus, joined me. 'She's afraid that there's too much of Ma coming out in me and she's not happy about it,' Yasmin muttered under her breath.

'What do you mean?' I asked.

Yasmin shrugged. She fell silent. I felt as though I was on the verge of some interesting revelation.

Nana had heard Yasmin's comment. 'Don't pay any attention to her,' she snapped.

I paid attention when I was told to, but paid even more attention when I was told not to, because I had discovered many interesting things this way.

'What were you doing with Cobus?' I asked.

'Mind your own business,' Yasmin muttered under her breath.

Nana studied Yasmin, who was walking ahead. There was a determined look on her face. Nana had told me that it would be in everyone's best interest to get Yasmin out of Sterkstroom, and that the longer she stayed the more likely she was to get into serious trouble. After what had happened in the park Nana seemed bent on doing something about it.

Nine

Mohammed's General Store specialised in dry goods and catered specifically to the African trade. The interior was filled with stacks of blankets reaching to the ceiling; billy-cans hung from the doorway in tight bunches and the three-legged cast-iron pots popular with Africans for outside cooking were propped up against the door; beads and colourful bangles festooned shelves stacked with rows of plastic shoes.

The general stores in town were quite similar, with their shelves filled with inexpensive, heavy, blue, cotton prints which the African women sewed into voluminous skirts. The cotton fabrics – serge, unbleached cotton and an off-white cotton twill – were the most popular lines.

In the rural areas the white-owned stores still had separate entrances and cubicles for African customers.

We were talking about this state of affairs one night when Nana said that it was no better than the time when Africans were required to do their buying through a hole in the wall without the benefit of viewing the merchandise. 'Remember, Delia? At Kruger's Butcher Shop the Africans had to stand at a cubicle which opened to the outside. They'd ask for two shillings meat and get a small parcel containing all sorts of rubbish, like sheep's hooves or . . . snouts.'

Nana didn't want to mention pigs' snouts in front of Papa because the very word pig was offensive to a Moslem.

'This country's gone to pot under the Afrikaners,' Nana complained.

'It is a legacy of the British,' Papa insisted. 'They did the same thing in India.'

'India, India! You're always comparing this country to India. The British had their faults, I'd be the last to deny that, but don't forget what your own people did to each other. The Hindus murdering their Moslem brothers and vice versa. Who can forget the atrocities committed by Indian upon Indian?'

Papa fell silent. After this he was a little more careful about making comparisons, even though Ma had agreed with him on this point about the British.

Despite the segregation and humiliation, shopping was still a major social event for the farm labourers. At Mohammed's General Store the African customers milled around the doorway or sat on the sidewalk, knopkierie in one hand, the other clasped around the bowl of a long-stemmed pipe, their conversation punctuated by cascades of crimson spittle aimed into the sand. The women usually did the buying, unselfconsciously peeling out their breasts when they paused to nurse the infants strapped to their backs.

The white farmers generally drove their black workers into town by lorry and dropped them off at the white stores, where they were forced to shop. At times like these Mohammed's General Store lost business.

Papa complained, saying that he didn't mind fair competition, 'but this . . . this is something I can't fight!'

It was because of these unfair business practices that the rumour about a recruiting office for black mine workers opening up in Sterkstroom caused so much excitement at home. We, however, weren't the only ones to interpret this as a good sign for business in an already depressed area.

'It means more people will be passing through the town,' Papa declared happily.

'They're closing the coal mines,' Nana reminded him.

'Oh, forget about the coal mines. Better things will be coming our way now.' There was talk about mining exploration on Boesman's Hoek. He had long suspected that the mountain would some day yield its riches. Whenever he drove through the mountain pass, he always talked about this. Daniel was in complete agreement; he sensed it too. Then, of course, there was a government proposal to complete the irrigation dam upstream. 'Things are going to get better,' he said, chuckling contentedly. 'This town is going to grow and we're going to grow right along with it.'

'The coal mine is what kept us going all these years,' Nana reminded him.

36

'Government aid kept the mine open. Our taxes supported it.'

Nana sighed. There was no use arguing when he was fired up in this way. 'Man, your husband has all these high hopes,' she told Ma. 'He's floating somewhere up there,' she pointed to the sky. 'You know what they say. The higher you go, the harder you fall.'

'Sterkstroom will be the new railway junction for this area.' Papa was so exhilarated, he could speak of nothing else.

Ma watched all these goings-on with a strange remoteness. Lately, she had become increasingly frustrated. 'Our lives,' she said to Nana one day, 'are so small and so limited, each day exactly like the next.'

Nana had listened in silence, her brow furrowed.

Ten

The winter that year was bitterly cold. In areas protected from the sun's rays, frost remained on the ground. Water pipes froze and burst. Each night before going to bed, Ma built a large fire in the kitchen stove, but the old building was designed to permit draughts, not to exclude them, and by morning the house was so cold that none of us relished getting up.

It was during this spell of cold weather that the response arrived from Miss Jones, the headmistress at the privately run school for Coloured and Indian girls located near East London.

'Where will we get the money?' Ma asked after a sleepless night of worry and anxiety.

'We'll find it somewhere. Tell Miss Jones we'll see her,' Papa said, having resigned himself to the fact that they could no longer keep Yasmin at home.

'The money, Abdul. Where will we get the money?'

Papa sighed. 'I don't know, but if something should happen to me, at least one of the girls will have an education. It'll probably be the only legacy I can leave her.'

'I thought you had plans for her,' Ma remarked.

'*Inshalla*, she's the eldest. I should make sure that she's settled. I've talked to some families who have sons of her age. Pity she's such a difficult child, and such a sharp tongue too. Perhaps an education will help to make the package more attractive.'

Ma listened in silence, shaking her head. Eventually she conceded that manipulating Yasmin would present a formidable task.

'Your mother is right,' he said. 'Look what happened to Baboo. No education and now he's working like a slave for his cousin, dreaming of some day becoming a famous cricketer.' He sighed. '*Inshalla*, if all goes well, perhaps we'll be able to educate both the girls.'

'This is the first sensible thing he's done in a long time,' Nana observed when Ma told her about Papa's decision. 'Sterkstroom is no place for a young girl. It's too easy to get into trouble. You know the devil finds work for idle hands,' Nana said, thinking of Yasmin in the park with Cobus.

'I'll inform Miss Jones that we'll see her on our way to East London next week.'

Yasmin was thrilled, and in the ensuing excitement she persuaded Ma to sew a new dress for the occasion. She selected a delicately printed blue crêpe from the fabric in the store.

'That's too grown-up for you,' Nana protested. 'Besides, it's cold for such a flimsy dress.'

But Yasmin persisted, and eventually both Ma and Nana gave in.

The drive of one hundred and eighty-five miles to East London was a miserable one. In the cold our breath soon iced up the windows. Shivering, we huddled under the comforter while Ma strained to see in the light from the headlamps.

'Are you all right?' Papa asked.

Ma nodded. 'Are you girls sleeping?' she asked.

'No,' Yasmin and I replied in unison.

'I expect Miss Jones will be asking quite a few questions,' she said, speaking over her shoulder to Yasmin. 'It would be a lot better if your Papa and I provided the answers.'

'Yes, of course.'

At this point Yasmin would have agreed to anything.

We reached Stutterheim at eight o'clock, just as the sun was coming up. Ma stopped at a garage and, while the attendant filled our petrol-tank, we took turns freshening up in the lavatory, where the shivering Yasmin changed into her new dress.

At first I was awed by Miss Jones, who met us in the lobby. Papa removed his hat and tried to generate an air of confidence, but it was clear by the way he squashed the crown of his fedora, then pounded it into shape again, that he was nervous.

'The education of the girls is not entirely academic,' the prim Englishwoman explained. 'There are several courses for their physical development too, as you can see from our playing-fields and stables.'

Papa's face registered his agitation. All the courses she referred to were a lot of rubbish. Where in Sterkstroom or in this country would she ever be able to use any of them, Papa had muttered. As far as he was concerned, an education involved reading, writing and arithmetic, not any of this other nonsense.

Miss Jones led the way to her office. She opened the door and swept in, the rest of us trooping close behind her.

She waited for us to be seated before nestling comfortably into her black leather armchair. 'I regard education as the promotion of a delicate balance between the mind and the body. *Mens sana in corpore sano*. A healthy mind in a healthy body. Don't you agree?' she asked, looking directly at Papa, who had his attention fixed on his hands.

There was a moment of silence. Then, realising that she was waiting on his response, Papa nodded his head and stored the statement for later consideration. We were seated in front of her desk and she pushed her small frame to the very edge of her padded chair, giving all her attention to Yasmin.

Apart from the initial glance, Miss Jones had ignored me completely. At first I wasn't bothered by this, because I was busy taking in my plush environment. Papa made several attempts to concentrate on what Miss Jones was saying. He nodded whenever she paused, but it was apparent that he wasn't really listening. Ma too had little to say, and so all the talking was left up to Miss Jones.

'Since we are catering not only to the Coloured community but also to the Indians, which of course includes those of the Moslem faith, we do provide food which is prepared in accordance with the Moslem religious ritual. The Moslem girls are served halal,' she said, 'just as the Hindu girls are served vegetarian meals. We purchase all our meat from a *bona fide* Moslem butcher in town. So you see there really is nothing to worry about.' Miss Jones concentrated her attention on Papa. She recognised, however, that Ma should not be under-estimated.

Her glance occasionally swept over me, but it was apparent that Yasmin had impressed her. I could see why. Yasmin looked radiant. I had, however, felt sorry for her in the flimsy dress and was relieved that it was warm in the office, where Miss Jones had a paraffin heater burning.

She clasped her hands under her chin and fixed her attention on Papa. 'Yasmin is a very beautiful young girl, perhaps a talented one too, and as such she needs a stimulating environment, one that will encourage her to blossom. I don't think your little town can do that. Am I right?'

'Yes,' Ma spoke up.

40

Miss Jones' glance shifted to her for a brief instant. 'It is imperative that young girls have ambition in life.' She smiled at Yasmin. 'It is this which provides the motivation and drive to get through school. A career is most important.'

Papa's expression tightened. I don't think he wanted some Englishwoman to tell him how to raise his daughters.

I studied his face. It seemed that he was not in the least impressed with Miss Jones. Before we left home, Nana had wondered aloud what a 'Miss' would know about raising other people's children.

It was hard to tell what Ma thought, though, because she had been in one of her silent moods ever since we left home. Yasmin, needless to say, was quite taken up and was hanging on to every word, her glance frantically darting between Ma and Papa, fearing that Papa would speak his mind and, in doing so, embarrass them all.

'Nursing is a very desirable career,' Miss Jones continued.

'No daughter of mine is going to be a nurse.'

'Well, what about teaching?' she inquired.

But Papa shook his head emphatically. We knew that Papa was being contrary because the suggestions were coming from Miss Jones.

She fell silent. She had listed the possibilities available for non-white girls and now discreetly dropped the subject.

'How much is this going to cost?' Papa asked.

'The fees do run high,' she said. 'There are many extras that have to be paid for.'

'How much?' he persisted.

She told him and he regarded her in disbelief.

'The school is a private one. Believe me, it's a much-needed institution for Coloured and Indian girls who have found them-selves in the same predicament as your Yasmin.' She glanced at Papa again. 'Why, we even have girls from as far afield as Mafeking and Louis Trichardt.'

I could tell from Papa's expression that this information was of little interest to him. Having already retrieved his hat from the side of the chair, he was ready to turn down the whole idea.

'We're quite willing to make sacrifices in order to give Yasmin a satisfactory education and get her out of the Sterkstroom environment.' Ma feared that the opportunity for Yasmin's education would be lost if she had to depend on Papa for a decision.

41

'I need to think about it.'

'I hope you won't take too long,' Miss Jones cautioned. 'We have only a limited number of places left.'

'You'll hear from me as soon as I make a decision,' Papa said coldly. 'What is the time?' he asked Ma.

'Twelve o'clock.'

'Too late for the market,' he muttered irritably. 'We might as well go home. There's no point in going to the city now.'

'What about a nice visit with Cassimbhai? You haven't seen him in ages,' Ma urged.

But he declined with a sharp 'No'.

'We'll be in touch with you soon,' Ma said to Miss Jones.

On the way home Yasmin and I listened to our parents speaking in incomplete sentences.

'I don't think so,' Papa mumbled, massaging his head.

'It'll be a good thing,' Ma countered.

'I don't like her.'

'That's nonsense. She struck me as a reliable person.'

'Too expensive. For that kind of money they should be eating biryani every day.'

Ma chuckled at his reference to the exotic dish. 'It's not that expensive. You said we'd find the money.'

'How was I supposed to know that it would cost so much?'

While the conversation continued in this vein, the unsaid hung delicately balanced in the air – innuendoes that the two adults only were supposed to understand but which were intercepted and interpreted for me by Yasmin. Ma was very persuasive and wore Papa down until he raised his shoulders in resignation.

Yasmin clasped her hands in glee.

Eleven

Yasmin's letter of acceptance arrived. She was required to register in January, which was the beginning of the school year.

She was thrilled by the news and indiscriminately bestowed smiles, hugs and kisses on all, including Nana.

Her high spirits were apparently infectious, because we were quite surprised at breakfast one morning when Ma unexpectedly declared: 'I'm going to have the house renovated, the outside painted and that damn backyard cleared.' In the ensuing silence all eyes turned on her.

My glance, however, darted anxiously between my parents. Lately, the anger between them had sputtered like an electric current dragging the rest of the family into its eddies.

'Where will we get the money? Already there is the expense of sending Yasmin away,' Papa protested.

'We don't need much. A hundred rands should be enough to do the whole house.'

'A hundred rands! Where do you think we'll get that kind of money?' he cried.

'I have a bit saved.'

There was another pause while Papa angrily and unnecessarily chewed his mouthful of oatmeal porridge.

'With all the talk about the government moving Indian traders out of the small towns, it would be best not to draw attention to ourselves, especially when we're right across the street from their church. You know yourself what's been going on,' Ma continued undaunted.

Nana was studying Ma from under her lowered lids.

'There's nothing wrong with this house. We've been quite comfortable here all these years,' Papa muttered.

'Ja, I know.' Ma's tone was cajoling. 'But let's face it. It needs

43

work. Take a look at the mess in the backyard. Look around you. See how the smoke has blackened the ceilings.'

While Papa sipped his coffee the silence intensified. Then he spoke. 'I suppose . . .' He was beginning to falter.

'Don't worry. I told you I have a little something put aside for a rainy day,' Ma said quickly, pouring his coffee.

'I think . . .' Nana started. Both Ma and Papa flashed her a warning glance, but she ignored it. Nana again was hurtling headlong into trouble. 'If they want to move us, they will. Spending money on this house is not going to make any difference. You'll only be throwing good money after bad,' she told them.

Ma and Papa both turned on her. They glared. For a moment she lowered her eyes.

'What do you know about this?' Papa demanded.

'You need material and labour. It's not that easy,' Nana said hotly.

'Stay out of this, Mum,' Ma snapped.

Yasmin, who had been holding her breath also, blurted out something unintelligible which was meant to ease the tension. I was praying that Nana would keep quiet. As usual, though, she was determined to have her say.

There was a flicker of concern in Yasmin's eyes. I had long suspected that there was substantially more to the relationship between her and Nana than either would admit. Nana had very strong family loyalties, often reminding us that blood was thicker than water.

'I can get whatever we need quite cheaply from the auction sales in Queenstown. Perhaps, with everyone helping . . .' Ma's glance swept the table and came to rest on us.

But this was too much to expect. Papa was more sceptical than ever. Nana shook her head, and although Papa was reluctant to follow her example, he just couldn't make any sense out of this urgent need to renovate the place.

'What's the point? Look what we have next door,' Nana said, gesturing towards the neighbouring house.

'I'll speak to Mrs Ollie.' Ma's tone had lost its edge.

Our neighbour, Mrs Ollie, kept her three jersey cows in the backyard. Although this was in violation of the town's health regulations, no one did anything about the flies or the stench. Mrs Ollie very wisely supplied us and several of the town officials with milk.

We had learned long ago that the round-faced, cheerful woman had many aspects to her character. She was an Afrikaner with a very strong sense of justice who dovetailed right into our lives.

Although Ma said she would talk to Mrs Ollie about the condition of her backyard, she never got around to it, because she was too busy planning and organising help for her own projects.

Two weeks later the shacks came down, leaving only the outside rooms intact.

I helped Papa to search through the rubble for salvageable material, but Ma stubbornly insisted that everything be carted to the dump.

'I want that old post,' he warned her as she started for the garage.

'It's useless; it's all rotted.'

It was true. I had spent countless hours watching the termites march off with the core, leaving only the husk. In Papa's present mood, however, I wasn't about to argue.

'You leave it alone. It's a good, solid piece of wood. We'll probably find use for it now. When times are bad everything has its use, even a dead snake,' he lectured, appalled by Ma's extravagance.

But she wasn't even listening to him.

'Daniel, help me to move it,' he said. But when he and Daniel attempted to lift the post it was so light that they both keeled right over. The beam that he had saved all these years had been cleaned out by white ants.

Nana had a hearty laugh. I had to keep a straight face though, because I was standing too close to Papa.

'So much for a dead snake,' Ma muttered. 'Throw it out.'

Next Daniel's home, the rusted Hudson skeleton, was unceremoniously tossed on to the donkey cart and hauled away.

'I hope you're satisfied that you've left Daniel without a roof over his head,' Papa remarked. It seemed that he was beginning to have second thoughts.

'He can sleep in the garage. There's enough room in the back for a mattress.'

'There's not enough room, Madam,' Daniel argued, offended that he was being treated with so little consideration.

'You should kick him out. Let him stay in the Location like the rest of us,' Gladys told Ma later, quite put out by the fuss Papa was making about Daniel.

'He can't stay in the Location. He has no papers,' she reminded Gladys.

45

'Then let him go back to where he came from.' She sniffed, imitating Nana's expression of disapproval.

Ma shrugged and walked away.

'Please, Ma, can we have an indoor flush toilet?' Yasmin pleaded. 'Like the ones we have at school. It's such a stupid idea to have a shower right beside that stinking hole you call a lavatory.'

'It's been good enough all these years, my girl. It'll be good enough now.' Nana quickly cut in to squash any grandiose ideas that Yasmin might have.

Yasmin ignored Nana and continued to badger Ma.

'Not now, Yasmin. I have a terrible headache.'

But Yasmin persisted.

'Okay, okay.' Ma put up her hands in a gesture of surrender. 'But first I have to see how we make out with Daniel's help.'

'If we were living in the city like civilised people, we'd have no trouble finding workmen. It's different in this God-forsaken hole.'

'You watch your tongue.' Nana glowered.

'It's all right, Mum. I've been thinking of installing an indoor toilet anyway.' At that point Ma would have promised anything to restore peace.

'Man, I don't know what's happening to this family any more.' Nana glared at Yasmin, then tucked her knitting bag under her arm and marched out to the arbour. In the shade of the grapevine Nana lamented loudly about the state of the world, and the curse of having children.

The day before Yasmin returned to school the indoor toilet was ready.

To mark the occasion the whole family, including Mrs Ollie, assembled while the first bowl of water was ceremoniously flushed away.

'This is an historic event. The first of its kind in the town of Sterkstroom.' Ma laughed as she depressed the handle and the water gurgled out of the bowl.

'Wait until the council cuts the water this summer, then I'd like to see how they're going to flush that contraption,' Mrs Ollie said to Nana as the two of them strolled towards the shop.

'Ja, but do you suppose they'll listen to me?' Nana asked, shaking her head. 'Best thing for them is to learn their lesson the hard way.'

46

Twelve

Most of the young people were leaving Sterkstroom. Moses Dlamini was one of the only two non-whites to gain admission to the Witwatersrand Medical School. Willem Arendse, his dream of Olympic fame dashed by the boycott, got married and moved to Queenstown. Cobus Steyn was at the University of Stellenbosch and Yasmin had left to begin her first year at the private school.

All the structural changes to the house were complete, including the glass-enclosed sun-porch where Nana and I spent evenings listening to the radio. Sometimes, when sports commentators discussed cricket scores, we thought of Baboo and knew that he would be up until the early hours of the morning listening to test matches being played in Britain, the West Indies and Australia, countries that he would only ever visit in his imagination. There was a lot of talk about television, and Nana said at least we'd have a window to the world.

'It looks fabulous,' Yasmin squealed when she arrived home for the short Easter break. 'Fabulous' was a new expression picked up at school. For two weeks she gave everyone a good dose of it, laughing as Nana grumbled, 'I never want to hear that word again.'

We celebrated my fifteenth birthday while Yasmin was home, and Papa surprised us with two bicycles acquired cheaply from Mr Marais, who had no use for them because his daughters had married and moved to Cradock. One had a lamp operated by a generator, the other a noisy horn attached to the handlebars.

'They look like leftovers from the Second World War,' Nana remarked as she examined the rusty frames.

'They're Raleigh bicycles. A good, solid, English make,' Papa informed her.

'Good? Solid?' Nana sniffed scornfully. 'This is post-war

rubbish, dumped by the British on every colonial market in the British Empire from India to Africa.'

Frankly, I didn't care whether they came from Timbuktu. A bicycle was a bicycle. I eagerly leaped on the one with the noisy horn and wobbled around unsteadily for a bit before getting the hang of it.

'You're still such a child,' Yasmin said scornfully.

Of course, she would have preferred to sit astride a horse in jodhpurs and riding habit. I mentioned this to her, and also reminded her that Papa wouldn't understand her lack of enthusiasm.

She gritted her teeth each time I went careening by, shouting 'Papa, Papa look!' But Papa had eyes only for one person, and it wasn't me.

Yasmin knew that Papa was disappointed by her lack of interest. 'How am I going to explain to him that I hate the damn bicycle?' she asked.

I shrugged. 'You'd better pretend to like it or his feelings will be hurt.' I wanted to make things difficult for her. In fact, I hoped that Papa would be very upset.

She was in the kitchen making a cup of tea later that afternoon when he broached the subject.

'Don't you like the bicycle?'

Yasmin's lowered lashes created great shadows beneath her eyes. 'Oh, Papa. Of course I like it. It's just that I'm so tired.'

I almost burst out laughing when Papa asked: 'Are you ill?'

'No . . . It's been tough at school. I thought I could rest while I was home.'

Nana happened to enter the kitchen in good time to hear this remark. 'That's all you've been doing since you got home. We've all been running circles around you.'

'If she's tired, she'd better rest,' Papa snapped. 'The bicycles will always be there.'

'It's all right, Papa,' she said, giving him a grateful look and ignoring Nana. 'Only you shouldn't have got us such expensive presents.'

'Nonsense,' Papa said. 'What kind of a father would I be if I couldn't spoil my daughters once in a while?'

Nana snorted loudly and left the room. 'I can't stand any more of this doting. For people who don't have much money, you're certainly throwing it around. First the house, now the bicycles.'

The next day Papa asked Daniel to help Yasmin. 'You hold the bicycle while she learns to balance herself,' he instructed, despite Yasmin's protests.

Although Daniel had little stomach for the task, he agreed.

Yasmin was mortified, but Papa stood by watching as she and Daniel battled back and forth down the street, Yasmin struggling to maintain her balance and her decorum, while Daniel strained to hold the bicycle upright as Yasmin wriggled away each time he accidentally touched her bottom. Nana and I were holding our sides. We hadn't laughed so much in ages. Yasmin was so angry that she wouldn't speak to me for several days.

Finally, after three days she was able to wobble along unaided while I raced by, gleefully shouting back encouragement.

'I hate the bicycle,' Yasmin hissed through clenched teeth. 'Cycling is common and undignified.'

It was at this time that rumours began to circulate about the new arrivals, a count and countess who had moved into the area. The townsfolk spent much of their idle time speculating about the VIPs.

Some hoped that with relatives in the neighbourhood the royal family might some day stop by for a visit. The townsfolk focused their energies dreaming up suggestions to beautify the town in the case of such an eventuality. One of the priorities would, of course, be the tarring of the main street.

In view of all this fuss Ma expressed her relief that the house, exposed as it was on the main street, was presentable, even though the gleaming exterior was only whitewash.

According to the grapevine, the count and countess had formerly owned a sheep farm in Australia and were planning to start a similar operation in the district.

There was much excitement and discussion about how one behaved in their presence. Yasmin, the font of knowledge, briefed everyone on the correct protocol.

'I'm not bowing and scraping to anyone,' Papa declared.

'Neither am I.' For once he and Nana were in accord.

'Royalty is special,' Ma informed them.

'They're only distant relatives,' Papa argued.

'The fact remains that they're still titled.'

Under Yasmin's expert instruction I practised my curtsey. 'Everything has to be perfect,' Yasmin said when we were advised that the count and countess were expected to call on the stores.

Since we were the only ones handling fresh produce, there was little doubt that we would be honoured in this way.

The entire day before the anticipated visit was spent dusting, sweeping, polishing and shining. Yasmin, who had no interest in the hard labour, showed no reticence about giving unsolicited advice.

At first Nana was reluctant to put herself out, but then, when she saw that I was going to be left doing all the work, she took charge.

'Hienie, Khoskhaz, who are these people that we are killing ourselves for?' Gladys complained.

'They are the Queen's family.'

'But they are not your family or my family . . .'

'Madam, she doesn't understand. She's never been out of Sterkstroom.' Daniel was scornful of Gladys' ignorance.

'What do you know?' Gladys demanded.

'Never mind, Gladys. Let's just get on with the work,' Ma said, trying to keep the peace.

By ten o'clock that night there wasn't a speck of dust anywhere. Nana finally straightened up and put her hands to the small of her back. Her braid, long since unwound, swung loosely below her waist. She checked the shine on the counter surfaces, then, satisfied that the job was done, packed away the cleaning equipment.

The sun was just coming up when we awakened at seven o'clock the next morning. It was a cool autumn day and Yasmin persuaded Papa to wear his good clothes. Despite his earlier reluctance to participate in what he considered frivolous activity, he entered the store dressed in the dark suit which he generally wore at funerals and weddings. The stiffly starched collar pinched. He pulled and tugged, stretching his neck to relieve the discomfort.

'Your Papa looks like a trussed turkey,' Nana said as she watched him fidgeting with his collar. Papa heard this remark and scowled.

Yasmin was dressed in a pale yellow dress and new black shoes with small heels and open toes which provided a tantalising view of her long, slender feet, walking with the lithe gait of an accomplished ballerina rather than the novice that she actually was.

I wore a white dress, patterned in green with little sprigs of red flowers, a trifle short and tight around the bodice, where I had filled out. Perhaps I was finally beginning to emerge from my chrysalis, I thought, as I studied myself in the mirror. Ma entered, looking radiant in her good dress, a powder blue crêpe which hung in soft pleats from the shoulders.

50

Nana, however, was determined to look her worst, in an old pink smock which was slightly soiled where she had deliberately wiped her hands to achieve the desired effect.

By midday the count and countess had not yet made their appearance and Papa was becoming more uncomfortable and disgruntled by the minute.

'It serves you right for pandering to Yasmin's whims,' Nana remarked when he made the mistake of complaining to her.

Yasmin was the first to see them. She was standing behind the counter when they arrived, accompanied by the member of parliament, Hermanus Steyn, and his son Jacobus, who was on holiday from university.

I recognised Cobus immediately, even though his appearance had changed. The pock-faced youth had changed into a young man, tall and muscular like his father, with the same brilliant blue eyes.

Nana's attention was on the count and countess, and she failed to notice the Steyns standing inside the doorway beside a tall stack of metal trunks.

The count and countess were both in khaki work clothes. Dressed like this they were indistinguishable from the other locals.

The countess smiled, grey eyes sparkling with amusement. 'My goodness me,' she gasped. 'I wasn't expecting a welcoming committee.'

Yasmin had no qualms about doing things and without any hesitation approached the newcomers; she curtsied, then politely introduced herself while Cobus watched intently.

My glance flew to him. It was easy for Yasmin to dismiss the incident with the doll, which in her opinion had happened a long time ago, but I was not so forgiving.

Ma was outside in the backyard and I noticed the way the older man was casting his eyes around the store.

Papa entered from the store-room, bowing stiffly, and, following Yasmin's instructions, went through all sorts of contortions to avoid turning his back on the count and the countess while attending to their needs.

'Oh, please,' the countess laughed. 'Treat us like any of your customers, Mr Mohammed. We're farmers now,' she assured him.

Hermanus Steyn remained in the background with his son, Cobus. Eventually, when he realised that Ma was not going to appear, he stepped forward.

Papa was cool but polite towards him.

The countess extended her hand to Papa. 'My name's Jill,' she said, introducing herself. The count stepped forward also.

'Wasn't she just fantastic?' Yasmin said in a daze after the visitors had gone. 'I'd love to be like her some day.'

'Not in this country,' Nana said quietly.

'I know. Still, I can't help thinking. Some day I'd like to be rich, and to do whatever I want to.'

Nana shook her head sympathetically.

'Perhaps I'll leave the country. Go to Australia . . . Did you see the colour of her eyes and her beautiful tan? I bet that's where she got it,' Yasmin said dreamily. 'I liked her husband. Wasn't he just ravishing?'

'Oh, yes,' I sighed.

'I must admit that they did seem like nice people,' Nana observed. 'But I suppose eventually they'll also change, and they'll become Baas Edward and Miesies Jill. After all, South Africa is the only country in the world where the term 'baas' is equated with colour.'

Before returning to school Yasmin confided that she had kissed a boy. She described in detail how his lips had lingered on hers, gently forcing her mouth open so that their tongues met.

'It's a French kiss,' she explained.

I listened attentively. I had never yet been kissed by a boy, but from what Yasmin said it certainly sounded very interesting.

'You'll understand it all one of these days,' Yasmin said, giving me the benefit of her experience.

I believed her, because Yasmin knew a great deal more than anyone else. As she spoke her face glowed with a radiance that seemed to illuminate her eyes, softening them with a sensuality that I had not observed before. I wondered who the boy was, for he had obviously made a big impression on her.

Thirteen

Yasmin was hardly back at school when Ramadan was upon us. During this month of fasting, like millions of other Moslems throughout the world, we were up before sunrise to prepare and eat the last meal of the day. Following this meal nothing could be consumed until sunset or for as long as a thread was visible to the naked eye – not a crumb of food or a drop of water could pass our lips.

'More pomp and circumstance,' Nana grumbled. 'All this fuss for one person.'

This wasn't quite true, because I fasted too, and Ma tried to keep up, but I had seen her eating when she claimed to be fasting. Nana kept all sorts of snacks in her room, until she found a mouse sharing her contraband.

I counted the days to the end of this gruelling period of deprivation. Papa's conviction that fasting was not only a religious necessity but also taught self-discipline was of little interest to me. My only interest was to get a fraction of the attention monopolised by Yasmin.

To take my mind off my growling stomach I watched the progress on the identical taffeta skirts Ma was sewing for me and Yasmin. These were for Eid, the day of celebration following the sighting of the new moon after Ramadan.

I wondered what my sister would have to say about the homemade garments. The last time Ma had sewn for us Yasmin never stopped complaining.

'Why do I always have to wear homemade clothes when other girls get to buy theirs from a store? Why do I always have to look like a frump? I hate homemade clothes!'

I was glad when Ma finally threw her sewing down and, placing her hands on her hips, fixed Yasmin with a stern glance.

'Now look here young lady, you seem to forget that your Papa

53

had to make great sacrifices for you to attend that school. In fact we've all made sacrifices, so I'd like to see a little more appreciation from you.'

That ended the complaints for a while, but I knew that my sister would soon forget this lecture and be back to her old tricks.

To me, it seemed that the dark blue taffeta shimmered in the light, constantly changing colour just like the Sterkstroom sunsets.

Outfitted in a pair of black pumps with a strap over the instep and wrapped in the swirling luxury of my skirt, I almost drove my parents and grandmother out of their minds as I pirouetted from one end of the house to the other.

'At least she's enjoying it,' Nana remarked when Ma complained. 'Not like the other one.' She studied me, then said, 'I think they'll look a lot better with crinolines.'

None of the fabrics in the store was suitable for this purpose. Nana suggested that some of the cotton netting might do. I helped her to cut small pieces from the roll and watched as she experimented until she found that the netting soaked in a sugar and water solution had the desired results.

Fourteen

'Daniel, you'll have to stay home to look after the house. We'll only be gone for a few days,' Ma said.

He fixed a woeful glance on her.

'There's no room in the car,' she explained.

At first Papa had argued on Daniel's behalf, but when Ma said, 'In that case I'll stay,' the issue was settled.

Yasmin's school was closing for three days, allowing the Moslem girls to spend the festive occasion with their families. The same concession was made for the Hindu girls at Diwali.

We were all looking forward to getting out of Sterkstroom for a while. Nana enjoyed visiting with friends and relatives, many of whom had long ago been moved out of North-End to Parkside, a Coloured township.

Papa's interests were Cassimbhai and a few of his other Gujarati friends, who always accompanied him to the Indian films at the non-white bioscope.

His real passion, however, was the big sprawling market place on Buffalo Street from where one could see the big ships docked in the harbour on the Buffalo River.

Yasmin visited her girlfriends to gossip and girl talk, or else they spent their time doing each other's hair and faces. None of this appealed to me.

I was drawn to the beach. It was all the same whether I was in the water or watching the waves from the Indian Ocean as they lapped against the white sand. The best area, the Orient beach, was reserved for whites, while the section set aside for Coloureds and Indians consisted of a rocky shoreline with intervals of sandy beach, an area still better than the one designated for Africans amidst the craggy rocks.

My favourite spot, however, was the rocky shoreline at West Bank. Here, water from the incoming tide was trapped between the rocks to form warm pools which harboured a fascinating variety of small crustaceans and plants.

When we arrived in East London, Cassimbhai and his wife Aishabhen were at the door to meet us, and although the sky was overcast, the new moon had actually been sighted in Johannesburg. Yasmin and I were elated. The prospect of another day of fasting was unbearable.

Hungrily, we viewed the assortment of dainties Aishabhen had laid out. Papa, who had been feeling out of sorts, had broken his fast earlier, but still he sniffed appreciatively at the luscious aromas in the kitchen. Aishabhen had cooked his favourite dishes; kitchri, a rice dish combined with lentils, and khuri, prepared from milk curds, spices and vegetables. The kitchri and khuri were served with branjal fritters and stuffed chillies. We ate in silence, nimble fingers picking at the rice and curds.

Papa inquired about Farouk, but Cassimbhai was reluctant to talk about his son. It seemed that Farouk had disappointed him by not coming home for Eid.

'He has exams. Universities don't close for Eid,' Aishabhen explained.

'Yasmin is doing well at school too,' Papa remarked.

I exchanged glances with Yasmin. It was evident that this was the match Papa was considering for her.

Cassimbhai was an older second cousin and a friend from the same village in India, and as such he and his wife were respectfully addressed as Bhai and Bhen.

Nana had said that Papa was a little envious because his friend had proved himself a more astute businessman.

'How's business?' Cassimbhai asked while the women exchanged news.

'Slow, very slow.'

Cassimbhai considered this response for a moment, then said, 'You should have come to the city.' He shook his head reproachfully. 'It won't be too long before all the Indians will be moved out of the dorps. The white-owned stores can't take the competition.'

Papa nodded wearily.

'We are the Jews of Southern Africa, hated and envied. Scapegoats, that's what we've become.' Cassimbhai shook his head reflectively.

'Yes, it seems we're hated wherever we go,' Papa agreed.

'We came with nothing in our pockets. All we had was our

56

determination and the smarts to succeed,' Cassimbhai said, tapping his head. 'I worked twenty-four hours a day every day of the week to get where I am now. I scraped and scrimped, putting aside every penny I could lay my hands on. Remember when we pushed that hawker's cart to Aliwal North because we couldn't get a licence in Jamestown?'

I knew that Papa remembered this very clearly. He often spoke about the time he and Cassimbhai were refused a licence because they were Indian and had to walk, pushing their cart full of merchandise, the hundred-odd miles to Aliwal North, where regulations were a little more lenient.

Papa nodded, although he felt bitter about the way things had turned out. They had both started with nothing. He had worked just as hard and had got nowhere while his friend had gone on to make a fortune. But in the end, he said, life was like that and that he bore no animosity towards Cassimbhai.

'All those Dutchmen sitting out there with their arms folded, coveting our hard-earned wealth. They want what we have. We worked for it, earned it and now we have to hand it over.'

'What has happened to you, my friend?' Papa asked, sensing that Cassimbhai was troubled.

'The Group Areas Board has struck here too. We are also to move.'

Papa was stunned. This was not what he had expected. 'Where will you go?'

Cassimbhai shrugged. 'Who knows. They've proclaimed this a white area and they've opened an area for Indians up on the flats.'

Papa shook his head. 'Is no one safe?' he asked. 'We're the only Indians in Sterkstroom. Where will they move us to? Surely they won't create a whole area just for us,' Papa remarked, hoping for reassurance.

Cassimbhai guffawed. 'You are my oldest and dearest friend, Abdul, and I'm going to tell you that you have your head up in the clouds. That's why you can't see what's going on down here. If they want to move you they will, even if it means creating an area specifically for you, just as they've done for the Indians here in East London,' he said, jabbing at the air.

Papa's mouth twisted into an expression of resentment at Cassimbhai's words. I was angry too. I didn't wish it on him, but it seemed that Cassimbhai would soon experience the vicissitudes of life. He would know then what it would be like to lose everything including your pride.

On Eid morning the menfolk trooped to the mosque for prayers while the women stayed home to prepare a variety of snacks for the well-wishers who were expected to stop by after the service.

Later on that morning I waited as my mother carefully unwrapped Yasmin's taffeta skirt, then held it up to the light for my sister to admire.

Yasmin gave a horrified gasp.

'You and Meena have look-alike skirts,' she explained.

'No one at my school would dream of wearing a taffeta skirt. It's okay for linings.'

Ma flicked the skirt to show how the material caught the light.

'Ma-a-a-a,' Yasmin moaned.

I took the skirt, held it to my waist and swirled around in an attempt to entice Yasmin while Ma stood to one side, her disappointment acute.

Yasmin noticed and relented. 'I suppose . . .' she began.

'Here, look at this,' Ma said, holding up the crinoline. 'Nana soaked it in sugar and water to keep it stiff.'

'What!' Yasmin cried, tossing the crinoline to the bed. 'How could you?' she wailed. 'What'll happen when the ants get hold of me?'

The ludicrous image of Yasmin being devoured by ants popped into my mind and I started to giggle.

'What are you laughing at?' Ma demanded.

But infected by my laughter, Yasmin joined in too. Ma threw her arms up in consternation. Later Yasmin tried one more time.

'Did you bring any other dresses, Ma?' she asked.

'Like which ones?'

'Oh, I thought you might have brought the one I wore for the interview with Miss Jones.'

'No.'

Finally, she had to wear the skirt.

'I see she's wearing it,' Nana observed.

'She's not a bad child . . .'

'Sometimes,' Nana muttered. 'But she always manages to get my gander up. I suppose one day she'll mature.'

Fifteen

The weeks dragged by. Things were quiet and I was bored. Weekdays weren't too bad, but I was beginning to get fed up with school too. Weekends were even worse, because there was nothing to do.

I had read every book in the house, including the dozen or so fly-encrusted romances that were strung up in the front window and had been there ever since I could remember.

One Saturday morning, for want of something to do, I volunteered to pick up the post at the post office.

I returned with the pile of letters. I had already checked and there was nothing for me. I wasn't expecting a letter, yet I always went through the same exercise, sorting through the letters in the hope that there would be one for me. But it was always the same. Nothing. Yasmin's letters were addressed to Ma. Anything for me was usually enclosed in her letter.

Ma riffled through the letters and picked up a large manilla envelope. She frowned and carefully scrutinised the government's identification stamp as though it would provide some clue to the contents.

There was a long silence while she read the letter through carefully. I noticed the sudden rush of blood from her face and knew instinctively that something was wrong. I waited for her to say something. Papa noticed too.

'What have you got there?' he asked.

'It's a letter from the Group Areas Board.'

There was a moment of silence. Ma looked up.

'What do they want?'

'They've assessed our property,' she said distractedly, scanning the typewritten page again.

'What? When?' Papa asked, startled.

'1,200 rands ... According to this, the house and shop are worth 1,200 rands.'

'Are they mad? When did they assess it?' Papa demanded.

'They don't say. But I think it was the time that Afrikaner came by to inspect the property about four or five months ago.'

'Why don't I know about it?' he asked.

'You were the one who spoke to him. Remember, you thought he was here to assess for property taxes?' she reminded him.

Papa had forgotten all about that incident. He nodded as it came back to him, his eyes narrowing. He had asked the man what he wanted but had got no answer from him. At that time they had thought nothing of the episode, but now it took on new significance.

I listened as my parents rehashed the incident, reading all sorts of relevance into how the man had walked, looked around and refused to answer questions.

'They're going to take over our home and our shop.' Ma was aghast. She glanced from Nana to Papa in stunned silence.

'Not while I have a breath left in my body!' Papa declared. Then he laughed. 'This is just another bureaucratic bungle. It's a mistake. We won't worry about it.'

'What if it isn't?' Ma asked.

He sat down heavily, considering her question.

'What are we going to do?' she repeated, thinking that he hadn't heard her.

'I don't know! But I won't let them take what we've worked for all these years! This is our house. We've built this business from scratch. There was nothing here when we arrived. We'll put up a fight. You just wait and see.' Papa's eyes darkened. Along his temple a vein stood out like a knotted rope. His clenched hand jerked open and involuntarily twitched as it rested on the top of the old rolltop desk.

'Fight with what?' Nana demanded. 'They'll come with bulldozers and flatten all of this whether you're in it or not. I've seen how the Group Areas Board operates. They declare an area white, then they come in and take over. They're not interested in owning these buildings. It's you they want out of this area. They don't care about your life or what you've put into this place. They don't care about anything except getting you out.'

'I don't think they'll break this down. It's a solid structure. I think someone wants it – probably old Faurie or van Wyk,' Papa said.

'We should have seen it coming, especially after what they did in the other small towns,' Ma said. 'Still, I think Abdul is right, we should put up a fight. We can't just go like lambs to the slaughter.'

Tormented, Papa leaned forward in his chair, drawing a hand over the bald patch on his head. 'What else do they say?'

Ma exchanged troubled glances with Nana. 'Nothing more, except of course that the property is worth 1,200 rands . . .'

Papa came upright so quickly that the old spring in the swivel chair twanged. 'It's worth a lot more than 1,200 rands. Look what we've done to the place. Look at all the improvements!'

'We'll discuss this when you've cooled off,' Ma said.

'Why steal our property. They can just ask us to give it to them for nothing,' he said with a touch of sarcasm.

'In the end they'll do just that,' Nana remarked.

Her words incensed Papa even more.

'Mum, please,' Ma muttered.

'This place is worth a lot more than 1,200 rands,' he continued. 'I can tell you. We built all of this from nothing. We sank all our money into the business and this property.' There was an angry pause. 'Go on, what else do they say?' he demanded.

'They've given us six months to find another place on our own, or . . . the alternative they present here is to move to McBain, which is a little less than halfway to Queenstown.'

'I know where it is,' he snapped. 'It's in the bush. A pile of bricks in the veld beside the road.'

'We've passed by it hundreds of times,' Nana said, 'never giving it a second glance. There's nothing there. Abdul's right. It's just a pile of bricks.'

'Dear Lord,' Ma sighed wearily. 'My home . . . Both my children were born here. I love this place.' She drew her hand across her face.

'We're not moving. This is our home and we're staying right here,' Papa told them.

Something really frightful had happened to the family. I stood to one side watching my parents and I wondered how such a terrible dread could ever be dispelled. The fear and anxiety of a future filled with uncertainty was unbearable.

Ma nodded. 'We'll see a lawyer. Abdul's right. We'll fight them. Why should we give up our home? Our livelihood is tied up here.'

They were at the lawyer's office first thing when it opened on Monday morning.

He told them that there was nothing they could do. It was a law, an act of parliament, that each racial group be confined to its own area. He said that we had no alternative but to abide by any decision the Group Areas Board made.

They came home angry and disappointed.

'That man is a *mangpara*,' Papa said as they stepped in the door.

Nana and I knew instantly that things had not gone right.

The adults talked of nothing else but this new threat.

'They leave one with nothing,' Nana sighed, 'not even your dignity.'

'What's happening?' I asked.

Ma shook her head wearily. They were too preoccupied to explain it all to me.

'What's going to happen?' I persisted.

'Everything will be taken care of,' Papa answered.

My parents and grandmother latched on to the phrase, taking refuge behind it whenever they became impatient with my questions. I wished that Yasmin was here. I missed her. I had no one to talk to now.

One afternoon following Mrs Dlamini's return from Johannesburg, she stopped by to see us. Nana made some tea and they stood around in the shop, anxious to hear about her trip because she had taken a parcel and letter for Baboo.

'Where were you staying in Johannesburg? Ma inquired.

'In Alexandra Township with Moses.' She shook her head. 'Here in the Location I have a home,' she said, dark eyes flashing, 'a brick house built for us by my husband before . . .' She swallowed quickly. 'Now my son lives in a tin shanty, worse than anything I have seen here in the Location. I hated to leave him. It would have been better for our boys to stay home,' she said. 'Johannesburg is a terrible place.'

There was a moment's silence while Ma quietly digested this information. She had suspected for a long time that Báboo too was having a hard time with his new family. 'It would have been a waste for Moses to stay here,' Ma remarked. 'And by now Baboo would probably have been in jail because of that Cobus Steyn.'

'I saw Baboo.' Mrs Dlamini shook her head again.

Ma's anxious glance sought hers.

'Moses went with me. The two boys were overjoyed to see each other. But we hardly had time to talk to him. That man that he works for is a slave-driver. Wouldn't even let Baboo talk to us for more than five minutes. The boy works hard, seven days a week. There is no time for cricket or anything else. Moses said he would go to see him again. You know how fond they were of each other. But they are both so busy now.'

'Did you see his place?' Ma asked.

'No. We did not go back to see him. That man he works for is a bad man.'

'It is his cousin.'

'Hmmm.' Mrs Dlamini pulled a face. 'He is still a bad man.'

'How does Baboo look?'

'He has grown tall since you last saw him. He is a man now, but I can see he is not very happy.'

'If it weren't for that damn Steyn boy, I'd get him back here.' Then she paused, remembering that any day now we might also be without a home.

Mrs Dlamini removed her glasses, cleaned them, then pulled a blurred picture out of her pocket. It was a photograph of Moses with two of his friends. She passed it around. The friend in the picture with him looked unsavoury, but of course I didn't say so to Mrs Dlamini.

She continued in a weary tone. 'He will have to find a place closer to the university. He is quite worried about the fact that he may be forced to transfer to a tribal college when the university finally closes its doors to non-whites. There are just two of them at the school of medicine now. Of course, there are other problems too. Not only is he a long way from school but few PUTCO buses run that route, so he either has to walk, and run the risk of being attacked by tsotsis, or else he has to get up at four o'clock to catch the train into town. This country is hard on its black people. It's even worse if you're a black woman. To think how I struggled to raise that boy. When they came to take his father . . .' she swallowed the lump in her throat.

Nana had told me that Mr Dlamini had been taken by the police. They came for him one night and charged him with sedition. He was never seen or heard from again.

Nana shook her head in despair. 'Man, it's amazing what our people have to go through for an education.'

'It will make my heart very sad for him to give up medicine. He likes what he is doing even though there are so many frustrations. He says when they are to dissect a white cadaver he has to leave the room, and then of course he misses the work and has to get the notes from one of the white students. If they are bad whites . . .'

We reflected about this in silence.

Mrs Dlamini sighed and clicked her tongue.

We had not told anyone about our impending eviction. It wasn't something that one talked about, but Ma succumbed to the urge to unburden herself to Mrs Dlamini.

'We might not be here much longer,' she told her.

'Why? What is happening?'

'The Group Areas Board . . .'

'Hienie, Tixo,' Mrs Dlamini responded, shocked.

'We had a letter from them.'

'Kaloku, this is madness. Where will you go?'

'I don't know. Abdul says we're going to stay and fight.'

Mrs Dlamini stayed on to talk for a while longer, the three women discussing all the possibilities. Listening to them I began to realise how limited our options were.

Sixteen

Three months later a registered letter arrived from the Group Areas Board. Enclosed was a cheque for 1,200 rands and a covering letter advising us that we'd be able to rent the house from them for an interim period while we made the necessary plans to relocate. Again, McBain was suggested.

'What can we do?' Ma cried.

'I don't know. We'll stay here. I told you we're not moving,' Papa said irritably.

'You better start finding another place,' Nana urged. 'One day they'll just bring their bulldozers. Cash that cheque. That's all you're going to get out of them.'

The cheque sat on the desk for weeks, because Papa would not take what they had offered him.

Business picked up over the Christmas season. Yasmin came home and once again the whole issue became topical. But there was little time to dwell on our troubles. We were so busy that we had to go on several short buying trips to replenish our depleted stocks.

'I wonder what's going on.' Nana said. 'I didn't think things would be this hectic.'

During the last two weeks before Christmas there was barely time to eat. The spurt continued right up to Christmas Eve and then we spent a quiet Christmas Day recuperating.

'This has been the best season we've had for many years.' Papa was almost his old self again.

'It's also our last season,' Nana reminded him.

'Perhaps things are turning around for us.' Ma said hopefully.

'Miss Harper says that you should always be on your guard when things go well. She says it's life's way of softening you for the blow that's to follow.' Yasmin was tired; she could barely raise her hand to help with the Christmas dinner.

'Sounds like that teacher is filling your head with nonsense,' Nana remarked.

Yasmin shrugged; that was all she could bring herself to do. She was much too exhausted to argue.

Papa tolerated the Christmas festivities because of Ma and Nana's Christian background. The usual Christmas gifts to the town dignitaries were delivered by me and Yasmin. The mayor, the sergeant of police and the town clerk were given the more substantial boxes of chocolates. The lower-echelon officials were given bottles of orange squash.

Each day Papa glanced at the cheque and then put it back on his desk. The lawyer had advised him to cash it. He warned that if it became stale the Board could very well come back with a lower offer.

Papa deposited the cheque into the business account and within a matter of days it was all gone, gobbled up by his many debts.

Nothing more was heard from the Group Areas Board and although the rest of us were lulled into a sense of complacency Nana remained alert.

Nana told me that she'd been through all of this before when they moved her out of her comfortable old home on the banks of the Orange River in Aliwal North to Hilltown, a flat, arid, treeless tract of land with not a hill in sight. Nana's anger rose. 'If I ever get my hands on a gun, I'll shoot the buggers when they come to evict us.'

Seventeen

One Sunday afternoon Ma left the house early. Nana and I were in the backyard when she drove off.

'I wonder where she's going,' Nana said.

I shrugged. Ma hadn't said anything.

She was gone for several hours, during which time Nana speculated about her whereabouts. Papa also had come out of the house once or twice to inquire after her. Nana told him that she'd gone for a drive, which was not what I'd heard her mumbling earlier. The name Steyn was quite clearly mentioned under her breath on more than one occasion.

And when Ma got home Nana was waiting in the backyard. I heard the car and stood by the backdoor. Neither of them seemed to notice me. The two were too busy arguing. Ma trying to push past Nana, who was barring her away.

'So I was right,' Nana hissed through clenched teeth.

Ma tried to push by. 'I don't know what you're talking about.'

'You stay away from Hermanus Steyn or I'll tell Abdul. Have you no pride?'

'I only went to see whether he could help us.'

Nana peered at her through angry slits.

'I had to try, Mum, I had to.' Ma's face was strained. 'All I did was ask the man to use his influence, but it was a waste of time.'

Nana was incensed. 'Dear God! You've turned this into a whorehouse! Just save Yasmin from the same fate!' She shouted, glaring at her daughter's retreating back.

Yasmin's exams were over and schools were closing for the June holidays. I went along when my parents picked her up on their way to East London.

We arrived at the school on Friday around midday. There was a message that Miss Jones wished to see us, but Papa was impatient to get to East London for the noon prayers.

'Tell her we can't wait,' he instructed the secretary, who disappeared through one of the doors and promptly returned to say that Miss Jones would see us right away. Yasmin joined us and we were shown into Miss Jones's office.

We listened impatiently to her preamble about the forthcoming vacation. 'It's a well-deserved rest before the difficult haul to the departmental examinations in December which will conclude her education at this school,' she commented, giving Yasmin a wry smile.

'We are aware of this,' Papa said testily. 'Is this the matter you wished to discuss with us?'

Miss Jones raised her hand. 'Yasmin is expected to attend a coming-out ball,' she said. 'It will be held when schools close in December.'

Papa's puzzled glance flitted from Ma to Miss Jones. 'What is a coming-out ball?' he asked.

'It is a tradition at this school,' Miss Jones replied. 'All the girls in their final year will be débutantes.'

'I don't know what this is all about.' He drew his hand across his forehead and shook his head.

'They will be graduating as young ladies, you know.'

Miss Jones's glance fluttered between Ma and Papa while Yasmin and I listened attentively.

'The occasion, of course, will also serve to present the eligible girls to the society in which they'll be making their contributions. Many important families from your community are expected. I'm sure you'll be interested in meeting them. You know in England this would be quite a social event. Débutantes are often presented to the Queen.'

Papa glanced at her in disbelief. 'I have no intention of allowing my daughter to parade herself. In fact, plans are already underway for her future, so there's no reason for her to attend.'

'What plans?' Ma demanded.

Yasmin fidgeted anxiously.

Miss Jones continued. 'She has profited from an education that has transformed her from a country bumpkin into a sophisticated young lady.' She paused, resting a condescending glance on Papa. 'She has reaped the benefits of ballet, elocution and deportment. We even indulged her with extra riding lessons because she felt she was not as good as the other girls. We went to a great deal of trouble to procure a special instructor for her while our own Miss Fitzsimmons was away.'

'Yasmin made no mention to us . . .' Ma said, glancing at Yasmin.

'I wanted to surprise you, Ma.'

'Well, you certainly have.'

'There's nothing wrong with her wanting to develop other skills. Many of the girls here are accomplished riders,' Miss Jones added.

'Why are you teaching her to ride a horse?' Papa demanded. 'What kind of a school is this?'

But before Yasmin or Miss Jones could answer, Ma interrupted. 'You mention a special riding instructor. Who is that?' she asked.

'He's one of the neighbouring farmers. As I mentioned, Miss Fitzsimmons, our regular riding instructress, is away and this young man, Andrew Jordaan, very kindly volunteered some of his time. We rent the horses from the farmers, and he makes a bit of pocket money when he's on holiday from Rhodes University.'

Fortunately, because of the exchange, I was the only one to notice that Yasmin had turned two shades darker at the mention of Andrew Jordaan.

'I had no idea . . .' Ma sat forward in her chair.

'Don't take it to heart, Mrs Mohammed. Yasmin has some very fine qualities, and of course the school has nurtured her like a delicate flower. A flower, you know, will not grow in a desert. It requires a certain milieu.' Miss Jones paused, then laughed. 'When you think of it, our job is much like that of a horticulturalist.'

Papa wasn't amused. 'What is involved in this coming-out ball?' he demanded.

'Only the cost of a long, white, formal gown,' she assured him.

Papa hesitated and Yasmin wrung her hands.

'Please, Papa,' she pleaded.

'Yes.' Ma spoke up. 'Yasmin will attend.'

Yasmin had informed Ma and Papa that she wasn't coming home for the September break because she hoped to spend it at a friend's home in East London.

'I can hardly wait for the holidays,' she had confided.

'I'm going to miss you.'

'I'll see you in December, silly. What about my dress, Ma?'

'There's a lot of time for that, young lady. Right now we have other problems on our minds, like the prospect of moving.'

'Why don't we just move to the city?'

'Oh, and do what there?' Ma inquired.

'We can open a store.'

'Where do you suppose we'll get the money?'

'Well, they paid you for this place.'

'The money went to pay the merchants. There's nothing left.'

'Oh,' Yasmin pursed her lips thoughtfully. 'As soon as I find a job I'll be able to help,' she said.

Ma shook her head. 'What kind of work do you suppose you can do?'

'I'd like to be a fashion model.'

'My poor child. You're a dreamer, just like your father.'

Yasmin's eyes narrowed. 'I'll be rich some day, even if it means leaving this country and going elsewhere.'

Ma sighed, hugging her. She held her tight, as though she was afraid of losing her.

Even Yasmin was a little sad about returning to school. It seemed that the family crises had drawn us all closer. There had been some wonderfully warm moments shared in the kitchen as a family. Remember this . . . Remember that . . . Our future did not exist. All we had now was our past and we dwelt on it.

It was like waiting at a station for the train to take away a loved one. I remembered the feeling I had had when Baboo left, or the feeling I got whenever I thought of losing Ma or Papa. Waiting to say goodbye to our home brought with it the same ache.

The days were short and cold, but when Yasmin left for school I often went to sit on the green park benches, ignoring the 'For Whites Only' signs. Here, I watched the squirrels darting in and out of the trees. Now and then they'd come to an abrupt halt a few feet away, black eyes blinking curiously while they sat on their haunches to observe me.

I had to get away from the house. But sitting in this peaceful environment I also had time to dwell on Nana's theory that trouble came in threes.

What else lay in store for us? There were so many questions and so few answers. Time was running out for me at the Sterkstroom Apostolic Primary School for Coloureds, but with so much happening I didn't dare think about my education.

It was a cold, blustery day in July and we were in the kitchen baking my birthday cake. There was an atmosphere of gloom in the house and Ma had had more than her share of trembling sighs.

70

'We don't want the batter beaten to death, just mixed,' Nana said dryly.

Ma's startled glance flew to Nana. Then she laughed out aloud.

'I was just thinking, it won't be long now before Meena will have to start her Junior Certificate,' Nana remarked.

I glanced up from the hateful chore of pitting the raisins, which were as hard as pebbles.

'I don't know what we're going to do about her then,' Ma continued.

'What about East London?' Nana asked.

'I don't know, Mum. I really don't know,' she sighed. 'I don't think I want to ask Aishabhen. I hate to take advantage of my friendship with them.'

'What about Jo'burg. I could stay with Baboo?'

'Don't be ridiculous. You can't stay with Baboo,' Ma said impatiently.

'Why not?'

'Because Baboo's a boy. Besides, he only has a tiny room which he rents from the store where he works. It can't be much, and who knows what mischief he's into. Jo'burg is a big city.'

Ma had worried about Baboo from the first moment he left Sterkstroom all those years ago. She told us that in a big city there were too many pitfalls for a young boy from a small town.

'The high school in Coronationville is a good school, and she could live with Lisbet.'

Ma thought about this for a while. Then she said, 'That's strictly a Coloured school.'

'So is the Sterkstroom school,' Nana reminded her.

'You know that they've allowed the children to attend this school because it's the only one in this area and we're the only Indians.'

'So?' Nana asked.

'In the cities the Africans, the Coloureds and the Indians all have their own schools, and they're not allowed to mix. I've heard that the Coloured Affairs Department will make no exceptions. They say the Indians have to attend their own schools . . .'

'Well, what's the problem?' Nana demanded.

'If we send her to the Indian school, where will she live? At least we know Aunt Lisbet in Coronationville.'

Nana shrugged. 'Well, I know for certain that she'll be in good hands with Lisbet. You'll like her,' she said to me.

I turned a pleading glance on my mother.

'What's the use? How can we send her away when there's so much happening. On top of everything else, we don't have the money.'

'The children must be educated, man,' Nana insisted. 'If it's money worrying you, I'll pay for her accommodation out of my pension. I don't need much.'

'Your pension is so small. How will you manage?' Ma asked.

'I don't think Lisbet will charge any more than fifteen rands a month.'

'That's practically your whole pension.'

'I'll have a bit left over.'

'Are you sure?' Ma asked.

Nana nodded. 'I'll write to her. The children must be educated.'

'I know, Mum. I regret that Baboo didn't get much of an education. When his parents died he was neglected. Perhaps things would have been different for him if we had done something about Cobus Steyn . . .'

'It's no use crying over spilt milk. Don't worry about Baboo; he has a strong back. He'll survive. He may not have an education, but he does have common sense.'

'Can I go to Jo'burg, Ma?' I pleaded.

'We'll see. I'll first have to talk to your Papa. You know what he had to say about Yasmin going away.'

'If he's smart he won't raise any objections,' Nana said, breaking the eggs and separating the yolks.

'There's also the old issue of halal food.'

Nana sucked the air through her front teeth. 'Don't worry about Abdul, man. What we have to do is find a way of getting her into school.'

'How?' I asked.

'The best thing to do,' Nana said, lowering her voice, 'is to have you reclassified Coloured so that you can attend the Coloured school. All you have to do is tell them a little lie when they ask you if you associate with Indians.'

'That's stupid. Her father is Indian.'

'They don't have to know that.'

'They already know. They have files and records on everyone.'

'Tell them that you've left him. They won't know . . .'

'This is ridiculous. I don't want to talk about it any more,' Ma said.

'It sounds terrible, Nana.'

'What do you care about the way it "sounds". We have to do something. In a few months none of this will matter, because we'll be out in the bush.'

'Ma, I don't want to change my classification. I'm Indian and I'm proud of it,' I said.

'Look, let me tell you . . .'

'For crying out aloud, Mum. All you and Abdul ever do is talk. I'm surprised that neither of you have varicose veins on your tongues.'

'Bah,' Nana grunted, turning her back. 'Meena, do you want an education or not?' she demanded.

Needless to say, I wanted an education, but not at any price. 'Papa won't like it when he finds out.'

'He won't find out unless you open your big mouth. Besides, these are unusual times.'

'I just want to be what I am.'

Nana dusted flour from her hands, then reached back to tie the bow which had come undone on her blue gingham apron. I helped her. When it was done, Nana turned around to face me. She gave me a long, hard look. 'What you are is a South African, and since you can't be that in your own country the next best thing is to be something that will at least give you an advantage. We're not trying to deny your birthright. The government has already done that. What we're trying to do now is to make the best out of a bad situation. Here, grease these pans,' she said, sliding the cake pans over towards me.

'I don't know why we're even discussing this. In the first place, Abdul will never agree.' Ma opened the oven door, giving us an over-the-shoulder glance.

'You don't have to give him all the details,' Nana said, wiping her hands on her apron.

'How can I not tell him about something like this?' Ma asked.

'It's quite easy. Don't move your lips. Anyway, why don't you first go to Jo'burg. See the school and then take it from there. Besides, it'll be a good opportunity for you to check on Baboo. But remember, the less said the better.'

I couldn't believe that Ma and Nana were saying these things.

'You're being as stubborn as your Papa, man,' Nana snapped. 'I told you you're a South African. That's the only thing that matters. The government's little tricks to keep us locked into our own corners won't make a damn difference when the time comes. What'll count then is who we are. Being black, green or blue will be an insignificant factor.'

'It's a matter of self-respect,' Ma replied, 'of pride, especially as far as her father is concerned.'

'We've lost both of those already,' Nana said.

Ma was still doubtful, especially in view of my reluctance. But Nana's argument was obviously carrying weight.

Ma told Papa that she wanted to go to Johannesburg to find a suitable school for me and possibly to enrol Yasmin in a college. She told him that she was anxious to see Baboo also. She made no mention of her plans for me.

'I'll go with you,' he said.

'It's going to involve a lot of running around,' she said, discouragingly.

'It's not good for a woman and a young girl to be on their own in Jo'burg.'

'I'll stay with Aunt Lisbet,' Ma told him.

'I'll come with you.'

The matter rested there. Ma worried that he would discover the plan to have me reclassified. When the time came for our departure, however, Papa backed out, because he wasn't feeling well.

'In that case I'll stay,' Ma told him.

'No, you'd better go, but be careful.'

'We'll be careful,' she said, caressing his head in a rare demonstration of affection.

Eighteen

'So this is Johannesburg,' I said, swivelling my eyes from one side of the street to the other. Tall skyscrapers with smoked glass façades reflected the blinding rays of the sun.

'Damn!' Ma ground the gears. 'I must remain alert.' But our licence plate with the prefix CEP which so proudly identified our origin also singled us out for abuse amongst the TJ licences.

Finally, we were out of the busy streets, but lost in a white residential area. Ma drove in silence while studying the signs, trying to gather her frightened wits. I called out the street names, tracing our location on the map. Eventually we found our way back on to the highway.

One of the signboards warned motorists to 'Beware of Natives Crossing Here', but someone had altered the sign so that it now read 'Beware Natives Very Cross Here'.

We arrived in Coronationville, where row upon row of box-like council houses lined the streets. Aunt Lisbet was expecting us and Ma gratefully set our luggage into the room which she had prepared for us.

Ma and Aunt Lisbet talked for hours after I had gone to bed. I could hear the drone of their voices while I drifted in and out of sleep.

A big weight had been lifted off her shoulders over supper when Aunt Lisbet had agreed to provide me with board and lodging for only fifteen rands a month. It sounded as though Nana had settled things with Aunt Lisbet before we got there.

Early the following morning Ma and I went to the school. We were both impressed with what we saw. Having made our decision, the next step was the reclassification.

The next morning we set off for Pretoria, the administrative capital where the government offices were located.

It took an hour and a half to get there in the DeSoto. Ma was irritable, saying that the old car had had its chips.

The morning was bright and sunny, the sky a clear blue shimmering expanse. We drove through jacaranda-shaded avenues littered with purple blossoms which popped under our wheels. The sun reflecting through the dense ceiling of branches left criss-cross patterns of light and shadow on the roadway.

Church Street took us to the government offices, where after some struggle we eventually managed to find a parking spot.

With a sense of panic I entered the dark gloomy hallway which led to the office in which we were to have the interview with the classification clerk. At the reception desk Ma stated the purpose for our visit and was handed several forms to be completed. Then we sat on the bench outside the office awaiting our turn.

Across the hallway a door was slightly ajar and voices raised in argument reached us. By leaning slightly to the side and craning, I was able to see into the room where an African man was standing, head bowed, before a white clerk.

He appeared to be completely intimidated by the abuse the white man was heaping on him. The official then instructed his black assistant to draw a comb through the applicant's hair and watched with perverse satisfaction while the assistant struggled with the fine-toothed comb.

'It's not going smooth,' the assistant remarked to his white superior.

'Please, Baas,' the man pleaded.

'How many pickaninnies you got?' the Afrikaner fired at the man.

'Five, Baas.'

'How big the oldest one?'

The man's hand shot out, palm up.

'Got you,' the official laughed triumphantly. 'Thought you could fool me, hey? You're a native, man. A native. You hear that,' he hissed. 'No way you going to be reclassified here. Come on, vat jou goed en trap, voertsek man,' he said, chasing the applicant from the room.

Humiliated, the African slunk away. My stomach seized into a painful knot.

There wasn't much time to speculate about the misfortunes of this poor man because it was our turn next.

We were summoned into the small, cramped office, where a

76

red-faced Afrikaner in his middle forties was shuffling through a pile of papers on his desk. My hands were clammy and I wiped them on my skirt, nervously wetting my dry lips.

'You remain silent,' Ma had instructed earlier. 'I'll handle the interview.'

The man looked up from his papers, and speaking in Afrikaans Ma stated our business. He listened in silence then fired a few questions at her. Finally, he asked about our association with Indians.

I watched Ma through the corner of my eye, heart pounding with anxiety.

'We don't associate with Indians. She's Coloured. All our friends are Coloured.'

His gaze was unflinching, menacing. Although Ma returned his gaze steadily, I suspected that she, like me, was quaking.

He seemed to be satisfied with her reply. He nodded, then turned his attention to me. I felt myself shrivelling under his unflinching scrutiny.

'I'm a Coloured,' Ma said.

'What about your husband?' he asked, returning his attention to her.

I wanted to flee, but Ma flashed me a warning glance. She hesitated for a brief instant, but to me it seemed like ages. Then she said, 'We don't live together anymore.'

'It says here that he's Indian,' the clerk said, jabbing at the file.

'That's right,' Ma said, the blood leaving her face. 'We're not together anymore and we want nothing to do with him or his people.'

Her voice was much too loud, I thought, feeling a knot of panic in my stomach. Ma had assured me that the official could do nothing more than say no. But I feared that the outcome would be a lot worse than that.

'She wants to live with my people.'

'Can she speak Afrikaans?' he demanded.

Ma was relieved that this seemed such an important criterion. 'Speak Afrikaans,' she commanded.

I stuttered and stammered, eyes mutely pleading with my mother, who, like the clerk, was expecting something profound. But I couldn't think of a thing to say.

The clerk's mouth twisted contemptuously as he continued with questions which I quickly dispatched in flawless Afrikaans.

77

He finished. I shuffled uneasily. He inked the rubber stamp, then banged the approval on the application and dismissed us.

'Are you all right?' Ma asked in the car.

I nodded, glancing at the crowd clamouring at the bus terminals. I tried to calm myself, to still the fears which had stirred terrifying thoughts, but my mind refused to focus on anything. I glanced at my mother and smiled timidly. Outwardly I remained calm, but inwardly I was in a turmoil. I felt debased and degraded by what had happened in that office. 'I'm all right. I'll be all right soon.'

We drove from Pretoria, with its Voortrekker Monument and Union buildings, all symbols of Afrikanerdom, and already I began to feel much better. The little flakes of gloom were peeling away, flying off through the open window. The process accelerated as we drove further from Pretoria.

I sat up and looked about me. The heaviness which had threatened to stifle me was lifting. Images collided. I had become almost immune to the beauty around me: the purple masses of jacaranda blossoms, the patterns of light and shadow on the street as the sun broke through the intertwining branches, the blue of the sky reflected in the windows. What a fool I had been to let myself be upset by that Afrikaner. My eyes and mind were once again in harmony.

I smiled cautiously. Disappointment, I had discovered early in life, was always on the heels of happiness. Things had to be taken slowly, one had to allow these feelings to envelop one, to give direction.

Nineteen

Vrededorp had been razed by the Group Areas Board, its inhabitants scattered. Baboo was now living in Fordsburg. He was overjoyed to see us and took us to his room, a small closet in the back of the store. There was no bathroom. The only lavatory was a public facility in the backyard.

But Baboo seemed not to mind. He worked long hours – sometimes fourteen hours a day with only a short break for lunch and supper. Because he lived on the premises and was accessible twenty-four hours a day, it seemed to me that he was much worse off than the other store clerks.

'Come home with us,' I urged. 'Cobus is no longer at school in Sterkstroom. Things may be different.'

But Baboo shook his head. 'No.'

'Do you still play cricket?'

He shrugged, dark eyes pained. 'One of these days.'

Ma was troubled because he looked so pale and sickly. 'Are you eating regularly?' she asked, scrutinising the room. A damp mustiness combined with the sharp pungency of urine filtered in from the outside latrine.

'Ja.'

'Where do you eat?' she asked, looking around for a cooking utensil.

'They have a small kitchen in the back of the store; sometimes we cook, sometimes Mohtibhen brings us food.'

'Baboo, are you sure you're all right?'

He nodded, thrusting an envelope into her hands. 'I want you to take this, Ma. You're going to need it when you move to McBain.'

'What is it, Baboo?' she asked, opening it. 'Baboo?' Her brows drew together. 'Where does this come from?' she asked, removing the wad of notes.

'It's money I saved.'

'I can't take this. You'll need it.'

'I want you to have it. It's not all that much – only 200 rands.'

'How could you possibly have saved 200 rands when you're only earning thirty a month?' Ma asked.

'I don't need much. And don't worry, the money isn't stolen,' he said, smiling wryly.

Ma flushed. 'I didn't mean to insult you, Baboo.'

'I know. I'd like you to have it,' he said.

He seemed so earnest, so intense, that Ma hesitated.

'Are you sure?'

He nodded.

She thought about if for a moment. 'I tell you what. Why don't I take the money and put it into an account for you. That way it'll be there when you need it. I won't use it. I can't, Baboo. It's your money.'

'I'd like to help.'

'Of course, and you'll get a chance to do so later.'

Baboo glanced away. Ma seemed troubled by the sad look which flitted across his face.

'What's wrong?' she asked.

'Nothing. I'm fine.' He turned away from her.

Both Ma and I sensed that he had lost his enthusiasm. It was as though he was waiting for the end of his life. There was no will left. He looked so unhappy that I couldn't help the feeling of uneasiness which passed over me.

Twenty

We spent another week in Johannesburg. Whenever possible we visited with Baboo, taking him hot meals and making sure that he had enough rest and was eating regularly.

On the Friday before our departure, Ma and I explored the Asiatic Bazaar in Fordsburg. Here whites and blacks rummaged through merchandise piled on trestle-tables which spilled over on to the sidewalks.

Elegantly dressed white women and their sari-clad counterparts rubbed shoulders on the crowded sidewalks. Cars crept through the streets at a snail's pace while drivers exchanged desultory comments with pedestrians who unhurriedly sauntered across the street to stores where faded banners advertised never-ending close-down sales at Moosa's Emporium.

Children lured customers into the stores by chanting: 'Cheap, cheap! Just come inside! Goedkoop, Goedkoop! Kom net binne! Cheap, cheap! Kom Mafuti Buya Wena!'

'Special price for you, Sir! Kom net binne! Two shillings for two or twenty-cents for two. Come on, Missy,' one of the children insisted, grabbing me by the arm.

Then, at twelve o'clock, the cry of 'Allah O'Akbar' shrilled from the minaret on the mosque and all life was suddenly siphoned out of the area. In a matter of minutes merchandise had been sucked back into the stores, sidewalks emptied and store fronts shuttered while Moslems gathered for prayers.

That evening Baboo again had to work late and so he sent over his friend Yusuf to take me to an early film at the bioscope in Fordsburg. After the film Yusuf and I stopped in at the Chez Amis café, which featured a jazz band.

Again, to my surprise, despite the strict segregation of races, I found whites and blacks surreptitiously squeezed into the small room. We found a spot on the floor and flopped down, sitting cross-legged.

The musicians returned for the second set. Their music awakened and stirred something deeply primal within me. Atavistic feelings probably sublimated for generations now surfaced. I could feel the blood rushing to my face and was grateful for the dim lighting. Mesmerised, I watched the bass player's long, sensuous fingers caressing the strings. He was oblivious to everything but the music, eyes half closed against the wraiths of smoke which curled up from his cigarette.

The euphoria, I soon discovered, was induced by tight hand-rolled *dagga* reefers furtively passed around. At first I was shocked, but the thought of Yasmin laughing at me, calling me a prude, soon gave me courage. I eventually found myself growing accustomed to the pungent smell of the reefers, taking deep breaths which left me with a pleasant feeling of light-headedness.

When the music ended at nine o'clock, part of the crowd drifted away. Yusuf located a table and ordered two Cokes. We were soon joined by four other people, three of them Indian and one African. Solly Karim was the oldest in the group.

It didn't take long for him and Yusuf to get into a discussion on Marxism, both conceding that they had not read the works of Karl Marx, or for that matter any other banned writer or philosopher whose ideology was in conflict with that of the government.

'Forget all this talking,' Solly said drily. 'Victory will come from warring, not from jawing.'

By this time a few others had gathered around the table and there was a murmur of agreement.

'Sometimes we have to talk. We have to convince people,' one of the newcomers said.

'You don't have to convince us, my friend,' Solly laughed.

'Ja. We still have to convince my people that from the beginning the nationalists have embarked on a deliberate policy to keep the blacks impoverished, a plan designed to keep them so busy scratching out a living that there would be no time to worry about politics,' Thomas Ndlovu said.

'Ja. But things are changing now. We don't have the old hang-ups about whites that our parents had. There's no "yes baas" and "excuse me miesies" from us,' Yusuf said, looking to me for support.

My wide-eyed gaze shifted from Solly to Yusuf.

'Well?' Solly demanded.

'I . . . I . . . I'm not sure,' I said.

'Why do they call you Meena?' he suddenly inquired.

'My name is Aminah.'

'That is the name of our prophet's mother.'

'But everyone calls me Meena.'

'Why? Aminah is such a wonderful name,' Solly said.

'Don't change the subject,' Yusuf interrupted.

Solly laughed. 'I keep telling you that the time has come to return fire with fire. Guns will do the trick. We need friends who can supply us with arms. You have to meet violence with violence, passivity won't get you anywhere with these people. They don't understand subtleties. You've got to speak their language.'

'No, I don't agree. If we do that, eventually the Cuban, Russian and Chinese presence will turn this continent into an area of superpower conflict. We'll become pawns in their struggle. The fight will no longer be ours but theirs.'

Ismail added, 'We have to have control of our own destiny. And that won't happen when we have Cuban and Russian guns.'

'It doesn't matter where we get our guns. No matter what we do, we're still damned. I say take what we can, where we can, and we'll deal with the consquences later,' Thomas responded.

'I agree,' Solly said. 'We can no longer settle for scraps from our own table. We need a united front. In small groups, isolated from each other, we might as well be castrated.'

They argued back and forth while I tried to analyse the strange fluttering that I felt each time Yusuf's hand touched mine or when our eyes met.

But it was getting late and, fearing that Ma would worry, I asked Yusuf to take me home. By the time we left it was almost eleven o'clock.

'Look after yourself, Aminah,' Solly said, grinning mischievously.

'You too,' I replied, shaking his hand.

'Maybe we'll meet again. Who knows, perhaps some day I'll pass through Sterkstroom, that one-horse dorp,' he teased.

Instead of taking me straight home Yusuf drove to Zoo Lake.

'I must get home,' I insisted.

'We'll just take a drive around Zoo Lake. You can't leave Johannesburg without having visited one of our best-known tourist attractions,' he said.

83

We parked and he coaxed me out of the car. 'We won't stay long.'

I hesitated, but there was a magical quality about the lake. By the time I got out of the car, my knees were like jelly and my heart pounded so furiously that I could hardly breathe.

Yusuf took my arm and we strolled to the edge of the lake. It was a beautiful, warm evening yet there were surprisingly few people around. The moonlight and the soothing sound of water lapping against the bank brought a warm rush of emotion.

Yusuf took me into his arms. I succumbed to that first touch, but then, startled and wary, I pulled away.

'Don't be afraid.' He drew me into the circle of his arms again. At first I was stiff and awkward, but he lowered his face and covered my mouth, his body taut with expectation.

My arms automatically slipped behind his head, our bodies knitting together, locked like two pieces of a jigsaw. One of his hands disengaged itself from my back and slid to the front, unbuttoning my blouse, which he slipped off my shoulder. He buried his face in my neck, gently lowering me on to the grassy slope. His head sank lower, hands unclasping hooks and lifting away the restraint of my underwear, lips searching, caressing, kissing, closing over the taut, expectant nipples.

My response was as natural as if I had done this a hundred times before. I buried my face in his hair, eyes closed in dizzying ecstasy. It was exactly as Yasmin said it would be.

Then quite suddenly I released him and pulled away. The spell was broken. Yasmin had come between us. Frustrated, Yusuf lay back breathing heavily, his hand dragging through his hair. I stood up, adjusted my clothing and did up the buttons on my blouse.

'Please take me home now,' I said.

Wordlessly, Yusuf got to his feet and followed me to the car.

Nothing was quite the same for me when we returned to Sterkstroom. I couldn't articulate the change but sensed it deep inside of me. Sterkstroom was somehow different. Not for a moment did it occur to me that I was the one who had changed. I no longer cared about staying here. It was a peculiar, disturbing feeling that left me unsettled.

'You don't know what it's like,' Nana complained. 'Your Papa's like a zombie. Daniel is as mad as a hatter. Your mother lives in some kind of fool's paradise, believing that everything will work out once we move. God alone knows what's going to happen to Baboo in the big city. Then there's your sister, with all her high-fangled ideas, and you'll probably be off to Jo'burg soon . . .' she sighed. 'I don't know what's going to happen to us. When you think you've reached the end, it starts all over again.'

'Don't worry, Nana,' I replied quietly. 'Things are bound to work out.'

A few weeks later we read in the *Sunday Times* that Solly Karim, arrested by the Special Branch a week earlier, had jumped to his death from the sixth floor of the building in which they had been interrogating him.

'He was so vibrant, so alive,' I told Nana. I had often thought of that evening with Yusuf and Solly. The recollections of Zoo Lake and Yusuf had been accompanied by a feeling so wonderful that it left me with this vague yearning.

Solly's death brought with it thoughts about the transience of life and my own vulnerability. 'Why would he have jumped?' I asked Nana.

'I doubt whether he jumped, child,' Nana said quietly.

But Nana's words made little sense. I was too far removed from the political reality of life in the big cities.

Twenty-One

The men from the Group Areas Board came on the day that Papa and Daniel had gone to East London. From the front door Ma and I watched them pulling up in the police van, accompanied by the sergeant of police, two constables and their dogs.

'What is it?' Ma asked. At first we thought that they had brought bad news about Papa. But when Ma saw the guns and the dogs, the blood drained from her face.

'What do they want, Ma?' I asked.

My mother shook her head. She didn't know either.

'These men are from the Group Areas Board,' Sergeant Klein told us, gesturing towards the dark-suited men. 'They . . . we are here to enforce your eviction.'

Ma's face was stark with fear. Then she looked at Sergeant Klein. It was all a mistake, she decided, expecting that the sergeant would rectify the ghastly error.

I thought so too. After all, he knew us, knew that we were harmless. Ma laughed mirthlessly, but there was no response from the circle of cold and dispassionate faces.

Nana, who had heard the commotion, came to investigate. 'What's going on here? Has something happened to Abdul?'

Ma shook her head.

'What's going on, Meena?'

'I don't know, Nana.'

Nana's questioning glance flew to the dark-suited strangers and then to the constables, finally coming to rest on Sergeant Klein, who was our only salvation. But he was studying the tips of his boots.

'We're locking up this property,' one of the men said.

Nana was aghast. 'Now?' she asked.

The man nodded.

'You can't do that. You're supposed to give us notice. We know the law. Besides, her husband isn't here. He's in East London,' Nana started to explain.

I shook my head.

'You received your eviction notice some time ago,' Sergeant Klein replied.

I exchanged troubled glances with my grandmother.

'No we didn't,' Nana put in.

'We have a copy of that letter.'

'But we didn't receive it,' I cried.

'The letter was registered and we have documented proof that you got it.'

I looked at Ma and it all became quite clear. Papa. It was the only explanation. He probably received the notice and destroyed it. Nana was right. He had been behaving very strangely.

'You've had enough time. Now move out of the way,' one of the other men said.

Throughout this exchange Sergeant Klein stood to one side, staring at the wall behind us.

'You've left us no choice,' the first man said. 'The matter is now in the hands of the police.'

The drumming of voices and the clattering in my head made it almost impossible to hear what was being said. This is Sterkstroom, I thought. This can't possibly be happening here. This is not a big city. People here are not evicted.

'We're not ready. We need time.'

'Go phone your Papa,' Ma instructed. Her bun had come undone; her large anguished eyes were turned on Sergeant Klein, pleading. Then her hands dropped to her sides in a gesture of helplessness. This was the image of my mother I took with me as I hurried away to phone Papa.

When I returned, two of the younger constables had pushed their way into the house.

'Get out! Get out!' Nana pressed her hand to her chest. 'Leave us alone!' Then slowly, her back supported against the wall, she slid to the floor. She was breathing heavily, her face ashen. Ma and I helped her to the door, where one of the younger men roughly pushed us outside.

'Pas op!' the sergeant cried, startled as Nana staggered. She would have fallen had Mrs Ollie not put her arm out to steady her.

87

In the passageway one of the young constables was dragging the blue stuffed chair from the bedroom.

'What are you doing?' Ma asked, horrified as he tossed it on to the sidewalk.

Nana covered her face with one hand, the other hanging limply at her side. Ma put her arms about Nana, supporting her while I righted the chair.

'Hienie, hienie, Khoskhaz!' Gladys shouted from the kitchen.

Ma helped Nana into the chair.

'Did you speak to your Papa?'

I nodded.

'Well, what did he say?'

'He said not to do anything. He's on his way.'

'Fine thing after the mess he's made,' Ma muttered. 'Keep an eye on your Nana while I go and see what's happening to Gladys.'

Nana's face was expressionless, one side pulling downwards. I sensed that something was wrong, but I didn't know then that she had suffered a slight stroke. I squeezed her hand reassuringly, dabbing at the spittle which dribbled from the corner of her mouth. The police would soon be gone and then we'd be able to move back in again.

'No! No! Please!' Ma's cry startled me out of these reflections.

I rushed to the kitchen. My mother was clinging to the arm of one of the constables, who was struggling to free himself. Ma held on as though her life depended on keeping him at bay.

Lying on the floor were pieces of broken porcelain.

'They belonged to my grandmother. Please leave them alone. Leave me alone! I'll do the packing. Why are you doing this to us, Sergeant Klein? Why? This is our home!' she cried.

'I'm sorry Mrs Mohammed, I'm only doing my job,' he muttered, and walked away.

But Mrs Ollie stopped him. 'What are you doing to these people?' she demanded. 'I know them. You know them too. They're not criminals. Why are you treating them like this? In God's name, man, what are you doing?'

'Look,' Ma cried, spreading her arms. 'My tea service, look at it,' she said, choking on a sob. Suddenly there was a loud crash from the bedroom. We all rushed to the front. On the floor were the fragments of Ma's precious porcelain basin and jug.

'Oh God, no!' Ma picked up the larger pieces, holding the shard with its delicate pattern of blue forget-me-nots against her cheek.

The other constable placed his hand on her shoulder, apparently intending to guide her out of the room, but she jerked free.

'I'll get her out,' Mrs Ollie said anxiously.

Sergeant Klein nodded.

Ma leaned against the dresser, clutching the piece of porcelain, tears streaming down her cheeks. Mrs Ollie led her outside. 'This belonged to my grandmother,' Ma whispered bleakly.

'Kom nou, Delia. Kom,' Mrs Ollie whispered, glaring at the police.

Out on the sidewalk Ma stared vacantly at our scattered effects.

Many of the townspeople had gathered. Some of them helped, others stood around, uneasy witnesses shuffling from one foot to the other.

'Are you all right, Mum?' Ma asked.

Nana nodded with great difficulty.

'I don't know what's wrong with her,' I said.

'It's the shock.'

'Come over to my place for a moment,' Mrs Ollie urged Ma and Nana.

Nana's head teetered. Ma frowned, her troubled glance studying Nana. I wrung my hands. I had seen that look in Nana's eyes, an expression of unspeakable terror.

'Take care of your grandmother,' Mrs Ollie instructed. 'I want to take your Ma inside for a moment. I want to get her a cup of tea. It'll help you to pull yourself together so you can think about what you're going to do.'

'I don't like the way my mother looks. I should get her to a doctor,' Ma said.

'Dr Uys is out of town. I'll get her a cup of tea.'

Some of the bystanders helped to pick up our scattered clothing, which I hurriedly threw into cardboard boxes.

Mrs Ollie showed Ma indoors to a chair by the window.

When the tea was ready she stuck her head out of the front door. 'Kom Meena, vat vir you ouma n'lekker koppie roibos tee.'

I dropped what I was doing and went to fetch the cup of tea for Nana.

'Dankie,' Nana said, accepting gratefully. Her mouth was not too bad now. She wasn't dribbling any more and I noticed that she was able to move her arm a little.

I held the cup to Nana's lips. Mrs Ollie had served the tea not in the enamel mugs they used every day but in her best china.

I returned the cup. Mrs Ollie and Ma were sipping their tea in silence, Ma with her head bowed, supporting the cup and saucer in her lap.

'Under the circumstances you might find this hard to believe,' Mrs Ollie said in Afrikaans, 'but we're not all like that.' She gestured to the police. 'I've been your friend for a long time. I know what you're going through. Hardship and pain are the same whether you're white, brown, black or green.'

'You've been a good friend to me all these years Sinnah.' Ma smiled sadly. 'Sinnah Olivier . . . I'd almost forgotten your last name. All these years you've been Ollie because the children couldn't say Olivier.'

I was about to leave when Ma said, 'Keep an eye on Nana please, Meena.'

Sounds from outside carried indoors and soon her eyes welled up again. They were emptying the store in the same manner as they had emptied the house.

'I'd better go,' she said to Mrs Ollie.

'You can store your stuff in my shed. The cows will be all right outside,' she said, accompanying Ma to the stoep.

'Thank you,' Ma said. 'Thank you so much. I'll leave the big items here . . . for a short while anyway.'

'What are you going to do, Delia?'

'I suppose we'll have to move to McBain. There's nowhere else for us to go.'

'That's ridiculous. The place is nothing but ruins.'

Ma shrugged.

Mrs Ollie sighed. She studied Ma. She didn't have to say anything. It was all there in her eyes.

Ma turned to go. 'Thanks for the tea . . . and everything,' she said, offering her hand, but the Afrikaner woman ignored her outstretched hand and embraced her, right there in the middle of the street with half the town looking on.

'Good luck,' she said.

'There's a phone call from East London,' someone called from the doorway.

'It must be Abdul. I'd better go.'

I rushed after her. Ma paused in the doorway to the store. The police were too busy carrying out their nefarious deeds to notice us. Ma took the phone and covered her ear to shut out the commotion.

She watched them with a disaffected air, as though she had cut herself off from all that was happening here.

In stunned silence she listened to the voice on the other end. One hand flailed behind her as she groped for a chair.

'What is it, Ma?' I asked.

'It's Aishabhen. Your Papa's had a heart attack,' she said, motioning for me to come closer.

I took the phone from her.

'The doctor says he'll be all right. The attack came on just after you called this morning. I think it was the shock of what was happening there,' Aishabhen said.

'Tell her I'll take the train. I'll be there tomorrow morning,' Ma said. Then, as an afterthought, she took the phone. 'Let me talk to him.'

'That won't be necessary,' Aishabhen told her. 'You have enough to deal with right now. He'll be fine.'

'Are you sure, Aisha?'

'Yes, I'm sure. He won't be in hospital for long. He's looking fine, Delia. Don't worry. He should be discharged tomorrow. He can stay with us for another week or so while he recovers.'

'I really appreciate this.'

'Are you all right?' she asked.

'Yes. My mother wasn't too well, but I think she's feeling a little better now. We'll be leaving for McBain in the morning.'

'Let me know if you need anything. Would you like Farouk to come and help you?'

'No, we'll be fine, thank you. You've been a great help,' Ma said. Drawing a hand wearily through her hair, she put the phone down.

With the weight of Papa's illness off her mind she was able to think a little more clearly about what we would do once we got to McBain.

'Will he be all right?' I asked, eyes bright with anxiety.

'Aishabhen says he was lucky it was a mild attack. She doesn't think it's anything to worry about. We'll call the hospital later,' Ma said. For a moment she watched the police carrying the merchandise out of the shop, then she sighed, shuddered and turned away. She walked away from the shop towards the house, changed direction and left the property through the side gate.

Most of our belongings and the stock from the shop were stored in Mrs Ollie's garage. The items which we needed immediately were packed into the old Buick, repossessed from Mr Erasmus.

Finally, Ma made arrangements for the transportation of the rest of our belongings to McBain by ox-wagon.

Mr Petersen, principal of SAPS, took us in for the night and Ma was able to take Nana to the doctor. Dr Uys' cursory examination revealed that Nana had had a mild stroke.

Gladys said that she would join us later when things were more settled. 'What about Daniel's stuff?' she asked.

'We'll leave it with you. I don't think he wants to come to McBain,' Ma said.

Early the next morning, before leaving the town, we stopped by the house. The doors were all padlocked.

Gladys stood on the front sidewalk until the car turned the corner at the end of the street.

We were leaving behind us not only our home but also a big chunk of our lives. Tears slid down Ma's cheeks as she watched Gladys's forlorn figure in the rear-view mirror.

I turned around for a last look. Both she and Daniel had been such an integral part of our lives, one of the many threads woven into the fabric of our existence.

'There's no use dwelling on the past. We have to go on,' Ma said, brushing the dampness from her cheeks.

'God, some day they'll pay for this,' I muttered.

'Not them. We're the ones who pay,' Nana said.

'What will happen to Daniel when he gets back from East London?' I asked.

'I don't know. I suppose he'll come to McBain . . . I don't know, Meena. I don't know anything, anymore.'

Twenty-Two

Papa didn't need to say anything. His guilt was quite apparent.

'Why didn't you tell us, Abdul?' Ma asked.

'Tell you what?'

'About the eviction notice.'

He sighed, drawing his hand across his head. 'I didn't want to worry you. I didn't believe that they would actually carry out their threat. I mean, why would they create an area specifically for us. One family. No one could be that stupid or inhuman.'

'You were wrong . . .' She drew her shoulders in, hugging herself as she gazed vacantly into the distance. 'Maybe they're planning to move the Asians out of Queenstown to this place too.'

'Twenty miles out of town?' he cried incredulously.

'That's nothing. They've done much worse elsewhere,' Nana reminded him.

Papa sighed.

Ma touched his hands, glanced into his eyes and realised how much he was hurting. 'We'll get through this somehow,' she said, stroking his hands.

'When will it end, Delia? When? All my life I've been kicked around. I'm tired now. Very tired.'

When Ma told Daniel that she had left his possessions with Gladys, he hopped on the first goods-train that stopped at the siding.

Conditions at McBain were much worse than we had expected. We picked through the rubble in order to see what could be salvaged.

Everything, including my schooling, was forgotten in the wake of this catastrophe. In my opinion the only important and relevant issues were those related to our survival.

With the aid of two labourers from a neighbouring village, Ma cordoned off an area in the store which we used as living space while the front of the shop was being constructed. It was an area large enough to hold three cots and a table. Papa and Nana each had one and Ma and I shared the other.

'To think that once upon a time we had a flush toilet,' Nana grumbled. 'And now we're reduced to performing our business like animals in the open veld.'

Some distance beyond the trading post, on the far side of the railway line was a siding with a water tower, painted army green, and two storage sheds. About 800 yards away were two cottages occupied by the Afrikaner railway workers and their families.

Our daily routine began with the drawing of the day's supply of water, which was hauled from the railway siding. Following this the meals were started on the primus stove. After breakfast everything had to be stowed, because animals from the neighbouring village strayed on to the property.

One morning, after we had been there for about two weeks, I caught sight of a familiar figure trudging along the dusty road. 'Isn't that Daniel?' I asked.

'Yes,' my mother said, shielding her eyes to stare into the distance.

When Daniel reached us, Papa asked, 'How did you get here?'

'I walked, Oubaas.'

'Why didn't you take the train?' he asked.

'No money.'

Papa shook his head.

'I'm so glad you decided to join us, Daniel,' Ma said.

'I will only be staying for two weeks, Madam.'

'But why? There's nothing in Sterkstroom any more.'

'It's a voice, Madam, which tells me not to leave the house. So I have to stay.'

'The house doesn't belong to us any more.'

'That's not what they have told me,' he said.

'Who told you?' Ma asked.

'The voices, Madam.' His tone was reproachful.

Nana tapped her head and exchanged glances with Ma.

'Where are you staying in Sterkstroom?' Ma asked.

'In my room.'

'Which room?' Nana asked.

'My room in the garage.'

'Don't tell me you're still on the property, Daniel.'

'Yes, Madam.'

'They probably don't even know that he's there,' Nana said.

'What's happened to Gladys?'

'She'll be coming here to work for you soon, Madam.'

'Oh, no.' Nana groaned.

Daniel shrugged disconsolately. He shared Nana's feelings about Gladys.

We worked hard to bring some kind of order to the property. Daniel was of great help and so were the three men from the village who exchanged their labour for provisions of tobacco and mealie meal.

Papa was happy about Daniel's company. The spring in his step had returned again. Ma was relieved; she had worried about him sitting on the stoep day after day, despondently massaging his head as though he had lost his will to carry on. But with Daniel back it didn't take long for them to pick up where they had left off in Sterkstroom.

'Madam, this is very bad,' Daniel said one day, putting his hands behind his back and inspecting the property like a general inspecting his troops. 'I shall write a letter to the CIA,' he said, taking a yellowed piece of paper from his pocket.

'What is that?' I asked curiously.

'It's a letter of identification from the CIA.'

'Let me see it.' Ma held out her hand. The yellowed piece of paper, she discovered, was a receipt for ten rands, issued by a Mr Bernstein for a bicycle Daniel had bought from him more than ten years ago. The scrap of paper had been scotch-taped along the folds where it had come apart from constant handling. She handed it to me. I read it, sombrely folded it and gave it back to Daniel.

Twenty-Three

Most of the perishable goods from the store in Sterkstroom had been disposed of. The rest of the merchandise was unpacked and dusted as we prepared to open for business.

Nana and Gladys were arranging the shelves. The open veld was encapsulated in a cocoon of hot air. In the distance the heat shimmered off the tracks. Outside, the only sign of life was a herd of goats resting under a scraggy thornbush.

'Good Lord, it's hot,' Nana complained, dabbing at her damp brow with the front of her smock. 'Do you know the Bible story about the plagues, Gladys?'

Gladys's stare was wide-eyed.

'You've read the Bible, haven't you?'

Her glance slipped away shamefully.

'Never mind,' Nana sighed. 'There's always something sent to torment you, whether you're a good Christian or not. Here in this country it's the white man, the heat and the snakes.'

'And the flies,' Gladys added.

'Ja. That's right.'

Gladys had learned that in this heat it was essential to conserve energy. Later, when it cooled down, she would pick Nana's conversation apart, chuckling quietly while muttering to herself.

Not long after Gladys's arrival Daniel, seized by one of his strange moods, had once again packed up and taken off. We weren't unduly perturbed, because we suspected that he had returned to Sterkstroom.

It didn't take Gladys long to settle in. To our surprise she soon made friends with the villagers.

'I'll be darned. I think she actually likes it out here,' Nana said. 'Have you noticed. She's quite a different person?'

I had noticed. Gladys spent hours conversing with villagers who stopped by. But it was Nana who was the first to notice that the old chief had taken a fancy to Gladys, often stopping by to talk to her. It was quite a sight, the chief leaning on his knopkierie for hours on end, like some English squire, while Gladys giggled and twittered like a young girl.

Within a matter of weeks, Gladys informed us that she would shortly become the chief's wife. A few weeks later she moved to the village. She continued to work at McBain, walking the four miles to and from work each day. By keeping her job at McBain she was able to feed the chief's children, half starved by the crop failure.

'Seems she's quite happy with her situation,' Ma commented.

'Hmmm. I hope it lasts. I think the only reason the old bugger took her as a wife was because she could feed his family.'

The chief had seventeen children from three wives, Gladys being the fourth. Ma observed that the chief's children filled the void left by her own children, who had gone to the city.

The younger children from the village came often. While she fed them and cared for them, not as much as a peeling was discarded from the kitchen; every morsel of food was saved for them. The rest of the time, however, she jealously guarded her position from the other villagers, often scolding them when they made a nuisance of themselves.

Then, with the cottage habitable, we moved in. Ma had used the money Baboo had given her to put a roof over our heads. As soon as she could, she vowed, the money would be replaced.

The front door of the cottage faced north, overlooking the store. The bathroom was a concrete pad with a little duct that drained the water outside, water which was still carried from the siding each day. A bucket was suspended above the pad to serve as a crude shower; the lavatory was still only a hole in the ground covered by a shack hammered together from planks taken off the packing cases.

We often reminisced about Sterkstroom and how well off we had been there. Ma hoped eventually to have running water, but Papa explained that it would cost too much to sink a borehole on the property.

None of the Afrikaner railway workers set foot in the store. Instead, they did their shopping in Queenstown. We depended mainly on passing traffic and the small trade brought by some of the surrounding villages, some of them almost five miles away. Business was extremely poor, but Papa optimistically clung to the view that the main road would eventually pass right by our front door.

It took a while to get used to the sound of jolting carriages, hissing steam and the occasional boisterousness of the railway workers, especially at night when everything was so quiet.

The passenger trains sped by, but during the course of the day several goods-trains hauling freight halted for water and coal. There was no need for us to buy fuel for the stove as we had done in Sterkstroom. Here, the gummy thorn trees made excellent firewood. Occasionally too we picked up pieces of coal along the railway tracks, even though this practice was outlawed.

Then, at the end of November, came the letter informing us that Yasmin would be home at the end of the week.

'You know what's going to happen when she gets here. We'll all be expected to run circles around her and none of the work will get done,' Nana groaned.

'Oh, Nana, she's not that bad,' I replied.

'We'll see, my girl, we'll see. A leopard doesn't change its spots.'

'We'll meet her in Queenstown on Friday night,' Ma said.

On the Friday afternoon we closed the store at five o'clock, and although I had volunteered to stay home, Ma wouldn't hear of this. Instead, she asked Gladys to keep an eye on the place.

Ma, Papa and Nana piled into the front seat of the DeSoto. The rear seat, removed at another time when we transported merchandise from Queenstown, had not been replaced. I opened one of the folding chairs, propped it up against the back of the car and made myself comfortable.

Twenty-Four

The first to spot her, I ran alongside the train to where it stopped, impatiently beckoning the rest of the family.

Yasmin stood in the entrance to the carriage, placed a cautious foot on the step and stared down at us. She hesitated, eyes large and luminous like those of a young doe. I saw the flutter of fear before her lashes came down and she took that delicate step into Ma's excited embrace.

She looked gorgeous. Her short hair suited her; the wispy fringe brought out those wonderful eyes.

'You've cut your hair,' Ma cried, holding her at arm's length. 'Such beautiful hair and you've cut it all off!'

Papa was waiting impatiently. Yasmin broke free of Ma's embrace and hugged him.

'You're as thin as a rake,' Nana commented drily, but she didn't deceive me for one moment. She was as happy as the rest of us to see Yasmin.

We lifted her luggage into the boot and she was about to climb into the back with me when Papa stopped her. He took the folding chair from her, opened it and climbed into the back himself.

'I can sit back there, Papa.'

'No, you sit in the front with your Ma,' he said.

I was disappointed. I didn't want to share her yet.

'Are you all right, Papa?' she asked.

Papa nodded. 'Things have not been that good lately. *Inshalla*, it can't get any worse. I'm so glad the family's together,' he said.

Yasmin looked away, disheartened. 'I should've been here to help.'

'It was just as well,' Nana told her.

'It doesn't matter. You're home now,' Papa interrupted.

I caught a glimpse of Ma and Yasmin's reflections in the rear-view mirror and was astounded by the resemblance. The two had never looked more alike than they did that day.

Ma spoke about the move to McBain and everyone chipped in. Before long we were all talking at once.

Yasmin's disappointment was acute when we arrived at McBain. It wasn't much and in this still atmosphere it was more desolate than ever.

Ma and Nana had both climbed out and were waiting for her. She slid along the seat, keeping her eyes lowered, afraid of what would be revealed there. I glanced at her. She looked up and for a brief instant again I saw that flash of fear.

'It's so nice to have you back,' Papa said.

'I'm glad to be home, Papa.'

She pressed her clenched fist into her back and Ma instantly responded to the small movement.

But she waved aside Ma's concern. 'It's nothing. A little stiffness from my trip,' she said, glancing around the property. 'God, it's so . . . so . . . what can I say?'

'What did you expect?' Nana demanded. 'The Taj Mahal?'

Bereft of a response, Yasmin stared after Nana's retreating back. 'She certainly hasn't changed.'

I marvelled at what was going on. Nothing had really changed. Somehow we had managed to pick up the threads again.

Ma, who had spent most of previous day in the kitchen preparing a superb feast for Yasmin's return, hastened into the house, inviting Yasmin in for her favourite – a glass of felooda, which was a special drink prepared from poppy seeds, agar-agar and rosewater.

Yasmin had no appetite. 'No thank you, Ma,' she demurred.

'But it's been a long trip. You must be exhausted,' Papa pressed.

'It's the heat.'

Ma marched ahead to the cottage while Yasmin lagged behind. She was in no hurry and sauntered, taking in her surroundings. Papa's fond gaze followed her as she linked her arm through mine.

'And you, little sister?' Yasmin asked. 'What have you been up to?'

I considered the question. 'Nothing much. It's only been six months since I last saw you,' I reminded her. 'What about you?'

'I can't remember the last time I did anything exciting,' Yasmin retorted, studying me. I stood with bowed head, using the toe of my sandal to draw geometric designs in the sand.

'You've changed.' Yasmin pounced on me as she had done when we were youngsters. 'You're different.'

'It's nothing,' I said, averting my eyes, wondering whether she'd guessed my secret. Later I'd tell her about it. She'd understand. She knew about these things; after all, she'd even predicted that it would happen. I thought about Yusuf and Zoo Lake, and sighed. I couldn't even count the number of times I'd picked up pen and paper to reply to his letter, but then found that I wasn't able to pour out my feelings for him.

'I know you.'

I hesitated briefly, then rushed on. 'I met a boy.'

'Where? Who?'

'When we were in Jo'burg,' I said, looking about me nervously. Yasmin's expression was incredulous. 'You?'

I could feel the blood rushing to my face and for a moment I regretted my impulsiveness.

'He wrote to me. He's really a nice person.' I thought about this for a moment, wondering how to phrase it, but there was no other way. 'I'm in love, but please don't say anything to anyone.'

'Oh, Meena. This is so exciting. What else happened?' Yasmin demanded.

'Nothing,' I said, looking away.

But Yasmin continued to stare at me, sucking at the truth.

'Nothing happened. We just kissed.'

Yasmin turned her beautiful smile on me, holding me at arm's length, exactly the way Ma had held her at the station. 'It's time, of course.' She inclined her head to one side. 'Yes, you have grown, my little dove. You're beautiful too, but I never doubted that you would be.'

I flushed. 'I haven't changed at all. You make it sound as though you've been gone for years; you've only been away for a few months.'

'So you kissed a boy. Did you sleep with him?' This was Yasmin, the *ingénue* at her best.

'You know I didn't,' I protested, slapping her hands off my arm. 'Let's go inside. I guess Ma and Papa are waiting for you.'

She stared at me in amusement.

'Why are you looking at me like that?' I demanded.

'So you're still a virgin.'

I walked away from her towards the tracks. I was so embarrassed; all I wanted to do was bury my head somewhere.

'Okay, okay.' She ran after me. 'I had no right to say that.' She caught up with me and, grabbing my arm, spun me around.

'Do you have to spoil everything?' I demanded, nearly in tears.

She laughed then, a quiet, husky sound developed since her last trip home.

'Okay, but I don't know why Papa doesn't find a husband for you instead of worrying about finding one for me. If you're not careful you'll end up being an old maid. You're saving it all, and for what? So you can sit on it?'

I'd heard enough. I walked back in the direction of the cottage. Yasmin followed, stumbling over the stones in her high heels.

'At least I don't throw it around the way you do!' I cried.

'I won't die wondering what it was like. *I* know,' she called out after me.

'Are you girls quarrelling?' Ma demanded when she came out to see what the fuss was about.

Yasmin shook her head while I pushed by Ma.

'Your Papa wants to talk to you.'

Yasmin came inside then, cautiously stepping across the threshold, and Ma affectionately took her arm.

'I'll show you the rest of the place later. It's not much, but I have so many plans. You can help me now that you're here,' she said.

Later, Ma showed her around the living quarters, taking great pride in what we had accomplished in this short time. She followed Ma into the bedroom.

'One of these days we'll sink a well and lead water to the house,' Ma said with suppressed excitement.

I was in the next room and I could hear Yasmin's high-heeled shoes tapping the concrete floor as she continued her inspection.

'What about a lavatory?' she asked.

'There's one outside.'

'Oh, Ma!'

'I know it's a little primitive.'

'A *little* primitive . . .'

'We have lots to do still. Right now it's merely a boxed-in pit. We'll build a flush toilet in the house like we had in Sterkstroom. But we can't do any of that without water.'

In the silence that followed I heard Ma's slippered feet padding across the room.

'I'm so glad you're home,' Ma said quietly.

'So am I,' but Yasmin's voice was dull and muted, tinged with anxiety.

102

Twenty-Five

'Trapped!' Yasmin muttered. 'Ma's tying me to her apron strings again,' Yasmin said, banging the teapot on the kitchen table.

I couldn't understand her. Ma and Papa were doing everything possible to make her feel at home.

'I sensed it the moment I stepped off the train,' she said. 'Life in Sterkstroom was bad enough, but it's like being buried alive here.'

'I thought you'd changed,' I said sarcastically, watching while she rinsed the teapot. She was making a cup of tea for Nana, and Nana was a fastidious tea drinker.

She lowered her eyes. 'Forget all my bitching. Old habits are hard to break.'

But I knew my sister. I knew there was something she wasn't telling me, something she was hiding. I questioned her, but each time I got really close to the answer, she changed the subject. It puzzled me, because it wasn't like her to be so secretive.

I had a feeling that she wasn't going to be with us much longer. She had plans. That much was obvious and I studied her whenever she wasn't watching, looking for clues. Whatever it was, she'd have to tell us sooner or later and I dreaded that inevitable confrontation.

We talked a lot the first little while, often into the early hours of the morning. I had missed her so, and I knew that she'd missed me too. Sometimes we got up during the middle of the night to sing and talk into her tape recorder, elaborate and affected conversations that had nothing to do with our real circumstances. They were fantasies in which we assumed the role of celebrities, Yasmin an actress visiting McBain and I the interviewer.

After a few weeks though we were all played out and her restlessness and boredom returned. Life settled into the old routine. Ma and Nana had managed to build a façade of normalcy which stifled her. She was right, of course; there really wasn't much

103

to do at McBain. We were isolated – no one to see or talk to outside the family. The arrival of a car sent us all scurrying to the store, eager to catch a glimpse of a new or a familiar face.

Yasmin seemed to mark the passage of each day like a stroke on a cell wall. Nana sensed her restlessness; there was a reproachful look in her eyes about this selfish attitude. Nana knew everything. It was impossible to hide anything from her. She had that uncanny knack of getting at the truth.

When we were young Yasmin and I always tried to outwit her, but it never worked. She knew everything! And when you least expected it, she pounced on you. Like that afternoon we caught Yasmin in the park with Cobus. I can still remember the expression on my sister's face.

Ma once said that Yasmin and Nana were more alike than either of them would admit.

I quickly dismissed these thoughts. I wanted to be like Yasmin. I didn't want to think back about the past. Those memories were much too painful. I wanted to concentrate on the future, but out here there didn't seem to be much of a future for any of us.

I wondered if Nana too might be bored. Perhaps this was why she became so cantankerous at times. When she had no one to argue with, she picked on Yasmin.

'How long does it take you to get dressed?' she'd ask Yasmin from the doorway.

'I'm putting on my make-up.'

'Make-up! Why would you want to wear make-up out here. Who's going to see you?'

And so it went. What did it matter how long she took. There was nothing to do anyway. If she took two hours to dress in the morning, it shortened the day by two hours. I wished that I could do that. But there wasn't much I could do to my face.

To keep us from going completely insane Papa brought home a box full of books bought at an auction in Queenstown. Most of these were old romances, as irrelevant to present-day life as those *Dick and Jane* readers were to our lives in Sterkstroom.

Miss Durant. I thought of Yasmin and the way she had interceded and taken that caning. There were other times too when she took the blame for something that I did and was punished.

I tossed aside the book I was reading. I'd read all of them anyway. Some of the better ones, like *Fountainhead* and two of

Lawrence Green's books, I'd read twice. At that point, like Yasmin I was all read out.

'I'm so bored,' Yasmin complained, joining me in the back of the house where I was sitting in the shade.

Nana, standing by the kitchen window, overheard this remark.

'You won't be bored if you do some work around the place,' she said.

'I've done my share,' she protested. 'There's nothing more to do.'

'You can always find work if you want to.'

'Nana, I've helped to put up fences, mould and fire bricks, I've raised walls and helped to put up the roof. I've had enough. Why couldn't they move us to a city?' she asked irritably. 'Why in heaven's name were we moved to this God-forsaken place?'

'How should I know?'

'This is the bloody end,' she cried, storming away. I watched her going and grinned as Nana pulled a face.

Ma and Nana talked about Sterkstroom constantly. All this talk awakened memories of the SAPS crowd. I told Yasmin that Willem was in Queenstown, Moses was still at university in Johannesburg, Dora was dead, Sarah worked for a white farmer and the rest of them had sunk into oblivion. She shuddered, obviously thinking that this might well have been her fate also.

Yasmin was thrilled when she discovered that Gladys' husband, the chief, owned a chestnut mare. I knew about the secret arrangements with Gladys to let her ride occasionally, and I discovered too that she paid Gladys with extra rations at the end of the week.

'If you give her that horse,' Nana said, 'we'll never get any work out of her.'

'She take good care of it; she's good girl.' Gladys startled Nana with this statement.

Yasmin was beaming triumphantly. I imagine Nana concluded they were both strange – kindred spirits. She always said that there was a little bit of the scoundrel in each of us. Perhaps, like everything else, Yasmin got more than her share.

We were all curious about Gladys' peculiar habit of disappearing on Sunday afternoons right after lunch.

One day when we saw her slinking around the back of the store, picking her way down the dirt track wearing only a grass skirt and

brief top, her face painted with red mud, Nana, Yasmin and I
followed.

The DeSoto was parked outside and we climbed in. I didn't have
a driver's licence, but out here it didn't matter.

We drove to the lay-by about a mile down the road and pulled up
in the shade of a large eucalyptus tree, where we waited.

Ten minutes later Gladys appeared and took up a position on
the shoulder of the road, about two hundred feet west of the lay-by.

Just then a touring bus came over the hill. To our amazement
and Nana's horror Gladys immediately started gyrating and
swaying. She leaped into the air. Her ample hips shuddered and the
skirt shimmered and sighed like the whispering of the wind
through the dried eucalyptus leaves.

At first we were stupefied, and then the penny dropped. Yasmin
and I started laughing so hard we couldn't stop. Nana had to jab
me with her elbow several times when the bus pulled up and the
passengers spilled out, crowding around her. I knew what she was
up to. I was laughing so hard that tears streamed down my face.
Nana was too amazed to react.

In the meantime Gladys posed, smiling and grinning at the
clicking cameras. She held out her hand and a group of Japanese
tourists eagerly emptied their pockets of loose change.

'Good God, woman! What are you doing?' Nana cried when the
bus had gone.

'I don't hear you say nothing. This is me. I do what I want,'
Gladys shouted, gesturing wildly. She was angry that we had spied
on her.

'Why are you making such a spectacle of yourself?'

'Spectacle? What spectacle?' She played dumb, but she knew full
well what Nana was getting at.

'I need the money from that bus,' Gladys told us plainly. 'You
don't pay me enough to feed all the children. I have to work for you
for many hours every day and for what?'

'You don't have to do this. Your husband's a chief. You are his
wife. You should have dignity.' Nana was incensed.

'Dignity don't bring food into the children's bellies when they
cry at night.'

'Ja. But it's no way for a grown woman to behave. Take a look in
the mirror and see what a sight-for-sore-eyes you are,' Nana said.
'You should have more pride.'

'I don't care about no pride or nothing. I care only about me and the children. The tourists, they pay me plenty. Look.' Gladys retrieved the coins stuffed into her tight bodice.

'That's not much!' Nana exclaimed, picking at the coins cupped in Gladys' hands. 'Most of these are pennies.'

'Today not so good. Japanese not pay well,' she shrugged. 'Sometimes very good.' She looked at Nana, eyes sparkling triumphantly. 'Anyway, my face very famous now. All those people go back to United States of 'merica with my picture.'

'Who do you think is going to do your work while you're traipsing and cavorting for the tourists in that silly skirt?'

Gladys merely shrugged her shoulders. She had switched off again. As far as she was concerned this matter didn't warrant discussion. She would continue to meet the bus and we could do as we pleased.

Yasmin thought the whole incident was funny. She particularly loved the way Gladys had handled Nana and the situation. We talked about this for days afterwards, still getting a good chuckle out of it.

We had an extremely hot spell. It was a little better than Sterkstroom, because here we only got the tail of the berg wind. Still, it was hot.

'It's hotter than hell,' Yasmin complained, retiring to a shady spot beside the house where there was a hint of a breeze. Nothing stirred between the hours of noon and three o'clock. Nana was lying down and eventually I dragged a folding chair over to join Yasmin. From this elevated position we could see the road and the occasional car passing by. We waved frantically and once or twice even got a response.

Few cars, however, wandered off the main road on to the dust road which passed by the store. Papa still hoped that a new road would be constructed to by-pass a dangerous railway crossing not too far from us where there had been several fatal accidents. He said that if they did this it would bring the main road right by our front door and business would pick up.

Daniel showed up a few weeks later. He had been turned off the Sterkstroom property. Ill, hungry and with no place to go, he had returned to us, this time with all his belongings, which he had stacked in one corner of the stoep.

'Seems like he's here to stay this time,' Ma remarked.

But we were never sure. Nana was right; he was madder than a

107

hatter and we were all that he had.

The store had increased its clientele. I thought business was beginning to pick up, but Nana claimed that there wasn't much money coming in.

'It's all penny and tickey lines: beads, bangles and mirrors.'

'At least it's better than nothing,' Yasmin said, mimicking Nana.

'How I miss Sterkstroom,' Nana sighed, ignoring Yasmin.

One morning at breakfast, Papa said: 'I hear that Prinsloo bought our store from the Group Areas Board.'

'Where did you hear that?' Nana asked.

'Daniel.'

'I hate to think of someone else living in my house,' Ma muttered.

A comment such as this always led into a session of reminiscing. Yasmin dreaded it. I could see the look of irritation on her face. But Ma's eyes had clouded and already she was digging back into the past. Yasmin fidgeted through breakfast and as soon as we could, she and I hastened to the village to borrow Blitzen.

I marvelled at the way the horse's condition had improved since Yasmin was home. The mare's coat was lustrous. Yasmin said that the brushing did it. I thought this was probably why Yasmin's hair was so beautiful too; without fail each night she brushed at least a hundred strokes.

The horse recognised Yasmin's scent and nuzzled the pocket where Yasmin usually kept a small reward for her.

I climbed up behind Yasmin, wrapping my arms about her midriff, face pressed against her shoulder. I enjoyed these moments with my sister. She loved riding, saying that it gave her a sense of freedom and power.

A track turned off the main road at right-angles, wandering across the veld, following the line of an earlier footpath. It led to the dry river bed which snaked around the village into the hills. Yasmin urged the horse through the donga along an easterly track.

The countryside was undulating veld, broken here and there by kopjes which appeared as mere specks from McBain. We rode through more dongas and gullies, all of them dry now. Spiral whirlwinds lifted the sand from one heap to another. The mare slithered down the wind-eroded embankments, shimmying and snorting while I held on for dear life.

The gum trees were covered with finches. I had never seen so many birds in all my life. Disturbed, they swooped into the air, blotting out the sun. Massing and turning, wave after wave of them returned to find new perches.

Black crows carked and bobbed on the skeletal trees, incessantly picking at the twigs and branches while they waited for carrion along the road where man and machine left a bloody trail of dead rabbits, squirrels and field-mice.

The short brown grass was matted, but ahead of us it shimmered and danced in silver mirages so that you could only look into the distance with slitted eyes. There were a few clouds in the sky and the oppressive heat portended a break in the long dry spell.

That night the humidity in the house made it impossible to sleep. Awakened by a clap of thunder, I saw Yasmin getting out of bed. She crossed the room to the window. Standing by the window staring out at the sky, she reminded me of a caged bird beating its wings against the bars. Once long ago I'd read about a bird that had beaten itself to death in this way. Would this be her fate also? She stood by the window long after the lightning had subsided, the rain coming down in steady sheets.

She tiptoed out of the room to the front door. I went to the window and watched the silver assegais plummeting to the earth, cascading down the walls, forming little lakes on the stoep before flowing to the parched ground.

Then I saw her on the stoep. Stark naked she stepped into the rain. The water glistened on her body. Sheets of distant lightning provided an eerie spotlight.

I rushed outside. To my amazement she was splashing and plopping through the puddles going through her old ballet routine.

'Are you mad?' I called hoarsely. 'Someone'll see you.'

'Come on. It's beautiful,' she laughed.

'You'll catch a death of a cold.'

'Nonsense. The rain is warm. It's beautiful,' she said, sensuously stroking her body. 'Come on, take off your nightie.'

I shook my head, waiting for her madness to end, but she continued her cavorting while the rain pelted down. 'Come on, Meena!' she urged.

I hesitated and, realising that I couldn't stop her, I thought I might as well join her. I dragged my nightie over my head and stood shivering for a moment.

After the first shock of the cold water I was surprised at how pleasant it was, especially after the unbearable humidity.

'Isn't it wonderful?' Yasmin grabbed my hand and dragged me off the verandah into the open.

I nodded, throwing my head back and allowing the rain to wash over my face. 'Yes.'

'You see. I wouldn't lie to you. You must learn to loosen up. You can't always take life so seriously.'

I laughed, shaking the water from my hair. We cavorted like two nymphs, oblivious to everything except the sheer joy of our freedom, uncaring about who was watching.

Exhilarated, we crept back into the house and dried ourselves.

My sister was exhausted and fell asleep instantly, while I listened to the clatter of the rain on the roof. Towards sunrise it subsided and the new day broke with an invigorating freshness.

Twenty-Six

On the day of the Debs' Ball we all helped with last-minute details. If this was only a débutantes' ball, what on earth would her wedding be like, I wondered.

The dress, a cloud of white voile, was ready and packed. She and Ma went by themselves. Papa changed his mind at the last minute.

'You go ahead and take her,' he suggested. 'I have no interest in such nonsense.'

But while they were gone, he paced the house, complaining about how quiet it was without them. They were gone for two days, because Ma wanted to spend a day in East London with Aishabhen.

We were in the kitchen when they got home, waiting anxiously for all the details. Yasmin said it was boring. Her escort had been some clumsy creature who had stepped all over her toes.

'I didn't think he did that badly,' Ma said.

'You weren't dancing with him,' Yasmin replied. 'This is how you dance the waltz. May I, Nana?'

Curtseying before Nana, she took her hand and whirled her around the kitchen in a stately waltz.

None of us had noticed Papa at the door. All attention was focused on Nana and Yasmin. Ma, who was usually alert, was too busy vicariously reliving the experiences of her own youth.

'The hall was a sea of white dresses and the boys all wore black suits. The girls were all escorted,' Ma said, interrupting Yasmin's comic impersonation of Miss Jones.

'What escorts?' Papa demanded.

Ma avoided his glance and Yasmin, stopped in mid-sentence, dropped into a chair. Ma had inadvertently surrendered an item of information that both she and Yasmin had agreed to keep from Papa, knowing what his reaction would be.

111

'The boys merely partnered the girls in a waltz,' she explained.

'How dare you parade her around a room full of people in the company of another man?' He slammed his fist on the table. 'You know that I am thinking of a match for her.'

'No, I don't,' Ma replied.

'With whom?' Yasmin demanded.

'Cassimbhai and I have been talking about you and Farouk.'

'Never!' Yasmin cried.

'They did nothing but walk around the room once and dance a waltz together,' Ma said, trying to smooth over the situation.

'Dance!' Papa spat out the word. 'Since when does a Moslem girl dance a waltz? What are you trying to do to her?'

'I want you to know, Papa, that I am not marrying Farouk.' But her protest again went unheard.

From time to time both Ma and Papa's angry gaze washed over me, sucking me into its eddy.

Papa was so angry he could hardly speak. Ma hurried out of the kitchen. The rest of us quickly took our cue from her and dispersed to various chores that suddenly required our immediate attention.

School was part of Yasmin's past now and she made no further reference to it. She seemed preoccupied and I wondered what was on her mind.

One Sunday afternoon, while she and I sat on the front verandah, I tentatively skirted the subject of our futures. She glanced at me in a strange way and I wondered again what she was thinking.

'Do you think I've changed, little sister?' she asked wryly. 'Come now, my little dove,' she persisted. 'Tell me.'

'What's the matter, Yasmin?' I asked.

'I'm in love,' she sighed.

I studied her for a moment. I should have guessed.

'With whom?'

'It's a secret.'

'Tell me,' I urged.

'Nope. If I tell you, everyone in the whole world will know.'

'I promise . . .'

But she laughed. Sometimes she liked to tease me, because it frustrated me to no end.

I shook my head and smiled. 'Nana's right, you are incorrigible.'

Ma and Nana joined us, and Yasmin tackled Ma right away.

'Why are you trying to palm me off on to Farouk?' her tone was angry and hurt.

'We're not palming you off on anyone.'

'It's only because I'm a girl. It's not fair and I won't be pushed into a marriage with Farouk.'

'Your Papa has only your best interests at heart. He wants to see you secure and happy.'

'I will marry when and whom I like.'

'You could do worse than Farouk.'

'Then let me!'

'It's easy to talk, but you make a mess of your life and all the chickens come home to roost with us,' Nana interrupted.

'If I were a boy things would be different . . .'

'Yes, and while we're on the subject of girls and boys, your Papa wants to know why you were taking riding lessons with that special instructor.'

'Papa wants to know?' Her tone was icy. She glared at Ma, ignoring the question.

'By the way, what's his name?'

'Andrew Jordaan.'

I waited with baited breath.

'And how old is this Jordaan fellow?'

'A few years older than me.'

'He must've been the young man I saw you talking to on the night of the ball.'

'Ja.' Her tone was matter-of-fact, intended to dismiss the subject.

But Ma was like a dog with a bone. She kept chewing on it. I could tell that she was leading up to something and that Yasmin was relentlessly being sucked into a trap.

'He must be quite something, giving up his free time so that he can teach you to ride.' Ma studied her for a moment. 'He was giving you free lessons, wasn't he?' she asked.

It was all beginning to close in on Yasmin. So this was her secret, I thought.

'Of course. Isn't that what Miss Jones told you?' she asked.

'I'm asking you.'

She was startled, but recovered quickly. She clapped her hands over her ears. 'All these questions!' she cried shrilly.

'I'm waiting for an answer.' Ma's eyes were like daggers, pinning her down.

'I told you,' Yasmin cried impatiently.

'Tell me again.'

'I don't know what you mean.'

'You know what I mean.' Ma's gaze was penetrating.

My glance shifted from Yasmin to Ma and back again. Yasmin gave an involuntary shudder.

'I don't know what you mean and I don't want to talk about this any more.'

'I want to know what's been going on!' Ma had grabbed her by the shoulders.

'Leave me alone!'

Ma's hands dropped to her side. 'I don't like the idea of a white man taking you for riding lessons. They have no respect for our people. Anything can happen and you could end up spending the rest of your life in jail. You know the law about black and white relationships. Does anyone accompany you?'

'No–o–o!'

'The two of you go out by yourselves?' Nana asked, dismayed.

'Yes! Yes! Yes! Are you satisfied now!' She fled then, almost bowling Gladys and Daniel over in her anxiety to get away.

Twenty-Seven

'I want to see the world. I'd like to travel through Europe, and do things I've never done before,' Yasmin said dreamily as we sat outside on the verandah one hot, summer's evening.

'Hmmm,' Nana mumbled.

'What sort of things?' Ma asked curiously.

'Surely this can't be all that there is to life?'

'We have a roof over our heads and three meals a day,' Ma said.

'Well, I can't believe that we were put on this earth just to eat and sleep.'

'A lot of people would settle for just that,' Nana said sharply.

I knew what it was I wanted, but I thought they'd all be too shocked, so I kept my mouth shut.

'What about you, Meena? What would you like to do?'

I shook my head and raised a shoulder.

'Come on, tell us,' Yasmin insisted.

I sighed. 'You don't want to hear about it . . .' I hedged.

'Of course we want to hear about it,' Ma said.

I thought about it for a moment, wondering how I could put my feelings into words. 'When I get to Jo'burg I'm going to get involved in politics.'

'Oh,' Nana said, raising a surprised eyebrow.

'It just makes my blood boil when I think of what happens to people like Karim. It also makes me ashamed to think that I'm not doing my share . . .'

Yasmin's mouth dropped. 'You mean you want to join one of those underground movements and get yourself killed or thrown in jail?'

'Your sister's right. Our jails are filled with radicals.'

'Doesn't it make you mad that we're out in the veld in the middle of nowhere, wondering whether we'll survive?' I asked.

'Of course it does. You know how we feel about it,' Ma said. 'But what good would it do us if we were in jail.'

'I agree with Meena,' Nana said.

'Mum, I wish you wouldn't encourage such nonsense,' Ma chided Nana.

Nana clamped her mouth shut and swallowed her retort.

Then, directing her next remark at me, Yasmin said, 'You must be crazy to think that being beaten or thrown from windows is something to relish.'

'You've always said you won't be pushed around,' I reminded her.

'Hah,' she laughed scornfully. 'Look kiddo, nobody pushes me around. I've learned to take care of myself. But I don't need a gun to do so. God, here we're talking about guns when all we need is a little more out of life.'

'There's no harm in wanting more out of life, depending, of course, on what it is you want,' Nana put in.

Yasmin shrugged indifferently. 'Whatever makes you happy.'

Her sarcasm was wasted on Nana. 'Happiness isn't something you can buy over a counter,' she said sternly. 'It has nothing to do with money or power. It's a good feeling that comes from knowing that you've done the best you can with your life, and that along the way you've reached out and helped, rather than trampled over, some poor straggler.'

Yasmin laughed.

'Let me tell you. Too many people are destroyed in the end by greed and selfishness,' Nana said.

Yasmin, who'd heard this before, sighed. 'I know that things won't be handed to me on a platter. I know that I darn well have to go out and get what I want.'

'Ag, you're not going to get any of it lying around the house like this,' Nana added, irritably.

'I don't intend to be here much longer.'

Ma looked startled. 'What do you mean?' she asked, peering at her in the half light of the verandah.

'What nonsense is this, now?' Nana demanded.

'I've heard that's it's not too hard to find a modelling job in Cape Town.'

'Who's been filling your head with this rubbish?' Ma asked.

'It's not rubbish, Ma. I can't hang around here for ever. I want to make money. I told you, I want to travel.'

116

But there was more. I could see it in her eyes and I wondered if it had anything to do with Andrew Jordaan. Was this the reason why she wanted to go to Cape Town?

Nana shook her head, arching an eyebrow at Ma.

'Ja. Look what's happened to Meena. She's not going to make anything of her life by sitting here either. What about her schooling? Is she going to rot here, also?' Yasmin asked.

'Yasmin!' Ma was appalled. She looked hurt and confused by Yasmin's outburst.

Nana sighed. 'You people of today are all so restless, so impatient. Everything has to fall into place right now.'

'That's right. I don't intend to wait either. You and Ma have spent all your lives waiting. And for what?'

'On top of it the Board came along and took what was left,' I added before Ma could reply.

'It's like standing outside a store window, looking in,' Yasmin said, glancing at me for confirmation.

I nodded vigorously. I could see the surprise in Yasmin's expression. She hadn't expected such belligerance and aggressiveness from me. 'Yasmin's right, Ma. McBain's no place for her, or any of us.'

'We'll talk about this some other time,' Ma said tightly. 'The elections are coming up soon . . . maybe we'll see a change.'

'Uh, hum,' Nana muttered, shaking her head. 'Those buggers are all alike. The good Lord just gave them different faces so we can tell them apart.'

'I'm not going to wait around for the elections in the hope that something may change,' Yasmin told Ma.

Ma was hurt and disappointed. 'We'll discuss this later,' she said grimly.

Yasmin's lips twisted into a wry smile. She glared at me and I felt a twinge of resentment. I wondered why she was blaming me. It was her own fault. I had nothing to do with it.

Nana said, 'You know that expression, Man proposes and God disposes?' She paused and then, struck by a thought, said, 'What if you can get a job in East London?'

'I don't want to be locked in some silly office filing papers all day long,' Yasmin snapped.

'Ag, Yasmin. Can't you for once be like any normal person. Why do you always want to be different?' Nana demanded.

'And don't worry we haven't forgotten about Meena,' Ma said, touching my arm. 'School is definitely not out of the question. We've already made arrangements in Jo'burg, but I first want things to settle down a bit.'

'Yasmin had better find a job. They're not that easy to come by any more. There are long lists of people waiting, willing to take what there is,' Nana added.

'Perhaps we can find you something to do in East London. Anyway, we'll talk about it later. I'm exhausted,' Ma said, getting up off the step and slapping the dust off her skirt.

She seemed relieved to have us all gathered under the same roof again and couldn't deal with the idea that any of us might be wanting to leave.

'If I go back to school, it'll have to be in Jo'burg,' I reminded her.

'*If?*' Nana asked. 'You ought to know that without an education there's not much you can do.' She glanced up at Ma for support.

'There's not much you can do with one either,' Yasmin chipped in.

'Well, I'm going to bed now.' Ma yawned. 'We can argue about this some other time. Coming Mum?'

'I suppose I'd better go to bed too, although at my age it's no longer pleasure but torture,' she complained, while Yasmin and I each grabbed an arm to help her out of the chair.

Twenty-Eight

One evening after we'd had Blitzen for the day, Yasmin and I were sitting outside, watching the sunset.

'If I hadn't skipped those art lessons,' Yasmin said, 'I might've been able to record some of these stunning colours.'

I smiled contentedly.

The orange orb suspended above the distant horizon had turned the bleached grass into a field of fire. As it dipped below the mountains it splattered the sky with pinks, softening the colours on the ground until the low thorn scrub spread out lilac shadows. Then, as it dipped even lower, those lilac shadows ran together in dusky hues.

'Well, it's getting late. I'd better return Blitzen. Coming?' she asked.

'No.' I stretched languidly. But when I saw her look of disappointment, I changed my mind. 'Okay, I'll walk you to the main road.'

Leading Blitzen, she walked beside me. We were silent, each preoccupied with our thoughts. When we reached the road, I stopped. 'This is as far as I'm going.'

She stepped into the stirrup and gracefully swung a leg over. The horse trotted along the shoulder of the road, its rider sitting perfectly erect. She was a good rider. She told me that Miss Fitzsimmons had often complimented her on her excellent posture. I could see why, I thought, as I watched her. I was really proud of her, but I was a little concerned about the situations she frequently got herself into. First it was Cobus, now it was Andrew Jordaan.

I stood watching her until she got to the turn-off. She looked back once and waved. I was deep in thought and oblivious to the traffic, although I had noticed a small, red sports car, which first sped by, then stopped, backed up and turned around at the lay-by on the hill. There was something vaguely familiar about it, but

119

Yasmin had already turned off at the track and so I didn't dwell on it at that point.

I strolled home at a leisurely pace. By the time I reached the house the sun had edged beyond the horizon and I watched with a sense of nostalgia as the last rays of sunlight dissolved into darkness.

By nine o'clock, Yasmin had still not returned. I made regular trips to the window to peer out, but there was no sign of her. Ma said that she was probably talking to Gladys and she didn't appear to be too concerned, because she was expecting Gladys to walk her home. Ma, Papa and Nana went to bed, but I stayed up to wait for my sister.

I don't know why I had this nagging feeling that something was wrong. The image of the red sports car came back to haunt me, although I still couldn't remember where I'd seen it before.

Eventually, when the rest of the family was asleep, I quietly slipped away, taking the car because I didn't have the courage to walk out in the dark by myself.

At the village Gladys told me that Yasmin had taken only a few minutes to remove the saddle and pat the horse.

'I told her. You no go by yourself,' Gladys said.

The fires in the village had by this time changed from faint flickers of dim colour to brilliant tongues of light in the darkness.

'She say there enough moonlight.'

I glanced at the evening star, which flickered like a large jewel set in a glittering bed of smaller gems. I could understand why Yasmin felt like walking by herself, but I would have felt a lot better had she allowed Gladys to accompany her.

'She want to think, maybe. Maybe you think something happen?' Gladys asked.

I shrugged. 'Maybe she's home by now,' I said hopefully, but decided to drive across the veld, following the narrow tracks through the trees.

There was a full moon and it was fairly bright out, yet I was unnerved by the immense silence. I drove slowly, bumping over the tracks and keeping my eyes open.

I was thinking about Yasmin and the knack she had for getting me upset when I picked her up in the car's headlights. She was by the grove of eucalyptus trees, and my heart bounced wildly when I saw her lying there. I came to an abrupt stop and leaped out of the car.

120

'Yasmin!' I cried, rushing over.

She stirred and opened her eyes.

'What happened to you?'

'Raped,' she said, lips twisting wryly as I helped her up.

'What!' I was incredulous.

She nodded. 'Cobus.'

The car! It all fell into place. I remembered now that the sports car was his.

'Are you . . . are you all right?' I asked, knowing full well that she wasn't.

'I'll live. Just very sore.' Her speech was slurred and she gingerly touched her face as I supported her to the car.

In the car I turned on the lights. She was a mess, her face dirt-streaked and swollen on one side. She had been crying; there were tracks down the inside of her cheeks. Very gently I touched the bruise on the side of her face.

She winced. 'He hit me.'

I quickly withdrew my hand.

'I'll survive, Meena. But please, I want you to promise me that you won't tell anyone, especially not Ma and Papa.'

I was flabbergasted.

'Please . . .' she pleaded, fingering her swollen lips.

I hesitated. This was too much to ask of me.

'Please, Meena, not a word . . .'

'But . . .'

'No buts . . . I know they'll blame me.'

'No they won't. They'll know what to do.' I knew what I wanted to do to Cobus! If only I had come with her, I thought, castigating myself.

'How did this happen?' I asked.

'I don't want to talk about it.'

'You have to tell me,' I insisted.

She turned her head away.

'I promise not to tell,' I said, gently turning her head so that I could look into her eyes.

She studied me for a moment, then made up her mind. 'All right then,' she said, dabbing at the blood and saliva which dripped from a gash on the inside of her lip.

She sat perfectly still for some moments, as though marshalling her thoughts. Then, when she spoke, her voice and face were expressionless.

121

'I was walking along here,' she said, 'deep in thought . . . not expecting anyone.' She let out a shuddering sigh. 'I almost jumped out of my skin when a voice said "Hello, Yasmin." It was Cobus. I was furious at the way he'd scared me. When I asked him what he was doing out here, he said he was on his way home.' She paused.

'I saw the car,' I said. 'A red sports car. He turned back at the lay-by. It didn't ring a bell until now. But it must've bothered me. That's why I had to find you.'

'God, imagine how scared I was to find him creeping around in the dark like a skelm.' She took another breath and thought about this for a moment, then continued. 'He offered to give me a ride home.'

'You said no, of course,' I said, heart pounding anxiously.

She was indignant. 'Do you think I'm crazy? I knew what he had on *his* mind. I realised that I was in danger.' She shuddered and her voice became tearful.

I put my arms about her. 'It's all right,' I soothed. 'It's all right.'

'It was so awful. I tried to get away, but he pinned me to the ground. I fought as hard as I could: I yanked handfuls of his hair, I scratched his face and I screamed. He hit me,' she said touching her cheek. 'I fought him off, Meena, honest,' she said raising her head, her eyes pleading.

I had no doubt that she had and I said something to that effect.

'I knew he was up to something terrible the moment I set eyes on him, and I don't know where I got the strength to fight him off, because I was so scared,' she said quietly. 'I tried to get away, but I was wearing these leather-soled shoes and they kept skidding all over the place.' Yasmin tugged at the ragged hem of her blouse and dabbed her eyes and nose.

I watched her, wondering what we were going to tell our parents. One look at her and they would know that something had happened. I waited for her to continue.

'I was out of breath by this time, and it was difficult to keep him talking. For one wild moment I thought that my fear was completely irrational. Why would he want to harm me? But when I remembered all the terrible things he'd done to us. I was afraid . . . more afraid than I had ever been in my entire life.'

As Yasmin relived those terrifying moments, I wanted to put my hands over my ears. I couldn't bear to listen, but I had to. She continued and I shared the anguish of every word.

'Then it happened. He caught hold of me, crushed me, pinning

122

my arms so that I could only wriggle helplessly. He dragged me into the trees over there. I struggled and screamed for help. He clamped his hand over my mouth, threatening to kill me if I opened my mouth again.' Yasmin raised her head to look at me. Her eyes were like large, tortured saucers.

'Let's not talk about this any more,' I said quickly.

But she continued, eyes bright and staring. Her voice rose and fell monotonously and I found myself having to struggle to keep track of what she was saying. I felt cold and dead inside.

When she stopped talking, I put my arms about her. We sat like this for I don't know how long. Then I started the car and drove home.

Yasmin went straight into the bathroom. She was there for hours and when I went in to see if she was all right, she was scrubbing herself with a brush. I took it from her, wrapped a towel about her shoulders and led her to bed.

Twenty-Nine

The rest of the family was shocked when they saw her the next day.

'What on earth happened to you?' Ma demanded.

'Blitzen threw me,' she said listlessly.

'I told you!' Papa cried. 'I told you not to get on that damn animal!'

'I'm all right, Papa.'

'Take her to the doctor,' he said to Ma. 'Something might be broken.'

'Nothing's broken,' she said. 'I just banged my face as I fell. I'll be all right.'

I listened in silence, watching Yasmin. I wondered how long she could keep the truth from Ma. Already Nana was studying her in that peculiar way as though she knew.

'Are you sure?' Ma asked, she wasn't quite satisfied, I could see her casting troubled glances at Yasmin. I wished Yasmin would tell them. At least they'd know what to do. I was no help. I was so affected by what had happened to my sister that I couldn't think straight.

She bathed constantly in an effort to cleanse herself. I tried to talk to her again, but she'd clammed up. Each time I mentioned it, her lips drew into a tight, angry line. For the first time I knew what it was like to really hate. I wanted to kill Cobus for what he'd done. Yet here I was protecting him with my silence.

For Yasmin it was a living hell. Not only did it affect her consciously but at night I'd get up to calm her while she thrashed around frenziedly, calling from the depths of her nightmare.

Would anything ever be the same again? Could she ever put the shattered pieces of her life together, I wondered, lying in the darkened room.

'I don't know what's happened to her,' I heard Ma saying. 'I wish I knew what was wrong so that I could help her.'

Ma questioned me, but I only told her about Yasmin's night-mares. When Nana studied me, I felt the blood rushing to my face. I wasn't good liar and she knew that I was hiding something.

'It's not like her,' Nana said. 'Something has happened and you're not telling us.'

'I don't know anything,' I protested.

Nana nodded, a perspicacious smile playing at the corner of her mouth.

With a start I wondered how she could possibly know. It was just a trick, I decided, just her way of drawing us out.

I was beginning to feel stifled at home and one Sunday about three months after this incident I asked Papa if I could go along with him to Oubaas Nel's farm, where he was to slaughter a sheep.

'No. You know I don't want you around to watch,' he said.

'I won't watch. I'll sit in the car,' I argued. All I wanted was just to get away for a while.

'Take both of them with you,' Ma said. 'It might do them good to get out. Everyone's been cooped up since we left Sterkstroom.' She was hoping the drive would cure whatever was ailing Yasmin.

Yasmin, however, refused to go. She had me worried. For the past few months she hadn't looked well. I just felt that I had to tell Ma or someone. She sensed this and cautioned me.

'All right,' I said reluctantly, 'but you need help.'

By the time we left for the farm, located at the far side of Sterkstroom, the sun had edged towards the midday sky, shimmering through a bright blue expanse of stillness.

We drove for miles along one of the back roads. I sat in the back seat staring out of the window. I knew that something terrible had happened to Yasmin as a consequence of being raped and I hoped to God that she'd speak up. She was morose and depressed. I guessed that she was trying to shut it all out of her mind. It was her way of dealing with the situation.

I berated myself again for not going with her that night. I prayed, eyes fixed on the heavens. Clouds gathered in the sky, drifting from one shape to another while I watched for a miracle, some sign that my feverish prayers had been heard. But I couldn't concentrate. There were too many fears, too many anxieties, colliding in my head.

When we neared Sterkstroom the occasional car passed by,

125

throwing up a cloud of dust and loose gravel against the DeSoto's pitted windscreen.

We could have taken a back road, skirting the town, but Papa took the main street. We drove by the familiar sight of the town square and he swallowed hard, passing the back of his hand over his dry lips.

If this was a wrenching experience for me, how much worse was it not for him, I wondered. The sight of our old house stirred so many memories, and for one exquisite moment I longed for the good old days. I sighed, knowing that all the wishing could not change a single thing that had happened to my sister.

When we neared the house, he slowed down to a crawl. We all leaned over to get a better look. The padlocks were off and the windows were curtained. Someone was living in our house. Funny how I still thought of it as *our house*.

'We took better care of it. Look what it looks like,' Papa said resentfully. He turned into the side road. The sign for Mohammed's General Store was still up, but the store was vacant. 'I thought you said Prinsloo bought it.'

'That's what I heard,' Daniel said.

'Well, there's no one there now,' Papa told him.

The windows were shuttered. There was no sign of life. He smiled and I could tell that he got some satisfaction from the fact that the store was still unoccupied. It would be a triumph for him if it stayed that way for ever.

He accelerated and, with his face grimly set, drove through the main street. The familiar sights haunted him and he swung off the main road, bumped over the railway crossing and sped out of town.

He was very quiet for the rest of the way. Daniel sensed his mood and, although he remained alert, kept his silence. Papa's sight was failing and Daniel was his eyes. He warned him about on-coming traffic, alerted him to the road conditions, and Papa adjusted his driving accordingly. There were times when he allowed Daniel to drive, but only when the roads were clear and he was sure that they would not be stopped by the police, since Daniel did not have a licence.

It was hot. The bare veld was baked to a crust, the ground criss-crossed with cracks which peeled back flakes of dry earth. Perched on the naked tree branches were the inevitable crows, their cawing an eerie sound in the vast stillness.

126

The expected bumper crop lay in ruins. The germinating seeds had pushed up above ground, shrivelled and died. Papa turned off on to a narrow stretch of tarred road about five miles from Oubaas Nel's farm. Here, the dust ate away the edge of the road leaving large, dangerous crevasses along the verge.

He slowed down when Oubaas Nel's farm came into view. 'I got everything,' Daniel said, 'a big cardboard box in the boot, the long knife with the black handle, a jug of water . . .' He glanced up as the car stopped at the last gate. Then, with an anxious look to the right and the left, he leaped out to open the gate.

A thorn tree, limbs grotesquely reaching for the sky, provided scant shelter for a herd of goats. Daniel, with a vigilant eye on the crows, waited impatiently for Papa to drive through. He slammed it shut the moment we passed through and ran for the safety of the car.

'If they hungry they eat your eyes,' he said in response to my curious glance.

'That's ridiculous, Daniel.' But he flashed me a tolerant look, wondering what I knew about any of this, before returning his attention to Papa's driving.

Oubaas Nel's home came into view. It was an old brick house much of which had caved in, leaving only a small part of the building habitable.

A dog barked at our approach and Aaron Arendse, Willem's father, who still worked for Oubaas Nel, directed us to the kraal, where Papa with Daniel's help selected a young ewe.

After some preliminary exchanges Papa found a level spot, scratched a depression into the ground, then removed a clean handkerchief from his pocket and covered his head before starting his prayer.

Daniel once said that he couldn't understand why Papa had to go through this ritual: dead was dead.

He shook his head impatiently because the animal, sensing danger, resisted and had to be pulled off its legs on to its side. Aaron came over to help, pinning its fore and hind legs. Papa then whet the sharp edge of the knife, continuing the prayer while he searched for the jugular vein.

The trapped animal bleated shrilly, its eyes rolling in abject terror while it awaited the inevitable. Papa parted the wool around its neck, then sliced into the flesh. I couldn't stand to watch any longer. My stomach lurched and I had to turn away.

127

'I told you not to come. Go back to the car,' Papa instructed.

'*La, illa ha Illaha* . . .' He started another prayer. The blood pulsed from the severed vein. The sheep's legs jerked and twitched. Papa held on to its head. The animal shuddered once more and then was still. An opaque film crept over the eyes, freezing for ever its terrified expression. It was all over. He released the head and the two men freed its legs.

I was so upset by the death of this animal that I vowed never to touch another piece of meat again.

Daniel, with Aaron's help, skinned the sheep and rubbed salt into the hide in order to preserve it for the tannery in Queenstown. The offal was gathered for Gladys and the eviscerated carcass was rinsed with the water brought with us. While Daniel trussed the carcass into the cardboard box, the crows hovered, lured by the scent of death.

At home it was hung out to dry in the bathroom, which was the coolest spot in the house. After two days, just as we were beginning to smell it, Ma instructed Daniel to cut it up.

On Wednesday night Ma prepared the sheep's brains for Papa. This and the kidneys were the only organs we saved. The rest was given to Gladys. My stomach was still upset and I couldn't face the meal.

Nana scowled when he cleaned off his plate with a piece of bread. 'How can you eat that?' she groaned.

Suddenly Yasmin uttered a peculiar guttural sound.

'What's wrong?' Ma asked sharply.

'I'm okay,' she nodded, but the next moment she leaped up and ran from the room.

The door slammed behind her and we heard retching sounds from outside.

I felt my stomach heaving. My regurgitated supper rose to form a lump in my throat. I tried hard to swallow it back, but I had to flee to the backyard, where I joined Yasmin.

She returned swaying slightly.

'You'd better lie down,' Papa advised. 'It must be the flu. We'd better get her to a doctor in Queenstown. I'll bring the car to the front.'

'Why don't you go into the shop?' Ma suggested. Her voice was lifeless. 'I'll find out what the problem is.' She got up and led Yasmin into the room.

Papa hovered, getting in the way, and Ma gave him a stern look.

Finally, he gave up and left the room to the women.

Ma hardly noticed Papa's departure. Her attention was fixed on Yasmin. I could see the apprehension in her eyes, a look of unspeakable dread, as though she had been preparing for this moment all her life. She took a deep, shuddering breath. 'Do you have your period?'

Yasmin shook her head.

'When was your last one?'

She hesitated.

I pleaded silently with her to tell Ma.

'I asked you a question.' There was something in my mother's tone which sent a shiver down my spine.

'I don't know,' she whispered.

Ma compressed her lips and glanced at Nana.

Yasmin turned her face to the wall, tears sliding down her cheeks.

'What's wrong with you?' Ma asked. But she knew the answer.

Yasmin no longer cared. The story poured from her lips.

The transformation in Ma was frightening to see. She writhed in agony, eyes fixed and staring as she grasped Yasmin's shoulders, shaking her.

'He forced me!'

Ma dropped her hands to her side. She was dazed. She clutched her head and with stooped shoulders unsteadily walked to the far corner. Suddenly she pounded her fists against the wall, crying out like a wounded animal.

Nana, ashen-faced, watched in silence.

Sapped of strength, Ma buried her face in her hands. We waited in silence, Nana holding Yasmin's hand, shaking her head in agony. I stood to one side, out of the way.

Ma fixed an accusing glance on me. 'You knew about it, didn't you?'

I gulped.

'I made her promise not to tell,' Yasmin said.

'Dear God, Yasmin, why didn't you come to me?'

'I was scared,' she whispered. 'So scared . . .' She burst into tears.

Ma sat on the edge of the bed.

'I was so scared, Ma.'

Ma reached down and cradled her head against her bosom.

'Oh, Yasmin, you should have come to us,' she rocked her in her arms. 'No one should have to go through something like this alone.

129

We love you. Oh, Yasmin, child, what is it with you?' Ma cried, anguished.

Thirty

I had my suspicions about what Ma and Nana were planning when I saw them huddled in earnest conversation. Yasmin had thought about this too.

'I don't want this baby,' she told me.

She already hated it and it hadn't even been born yet.

'I don't want it. We have to get rid of it,' she said over and over again.

Ma drew her into the circle of her arms, stroked her hair and tried to calm her.

'Ma, I want an abortion!' she cried, teetering on the brink of hysteria.

'We don't know yet,' Ma said, gaunt with worry. 'We have to find someone to do it. We can't have it done in some dirty little shack where you'll end up with blood poisoning.'

'I don't care! I just want it out of me.'

Ma took a deep breath and shook her head. She took Yasmin's face in her hands. Ma's eyes were dull and dark-ringed from weeks of sleepless agony. 'My dear child, you've been through so much,' she said. 'If only Meena had gone with you that night . . .'

'Don't blame Meena,' Nana said. 'She's suffered enough too. Let's concentrate on what we've got to do. Damn him into hell!' she cried. 'Dear Jesus, what are we going to do?'

I listened fearfully. It was as though the heart had been ripped out of my family.

Papa was devastated. He shrank into the shadows, leaving the women to deal with the situation. He had aged considerably. His shoulders were stooped and his eyes had a glazed look which had nothing to do with his cataracts. He seemed to be miles away, and we often had to repeat ourselves two or three times before he heard or understood.

Once the decision had been made for an abortion, Nana

131

telephoned a friend in Aliwal North. An appointment was first made with the doctor there to confirm the pregnancy. Nana was impatient. 'We know that she's three-and-a-half months. We don't need a doctor to tell us the obvious.'

Nana's friend Queenie also agreed to make arrangements with a midwife who knew about these things, although she had expressed reservations about the abortion, fearing that Yasmin was too far gone already. Nana, however, would not give up hope.

The Friday evening before the appointment in Aliwal North, I went into the room where Yasmin was stretched out on her bed, arms folded across her chest, eyes open unblinkingly fixed on the ceiling.

Stunned, I stood in the doorway for a moment thinking that she was dead. 'Yasmin!' I cried, shaking her shoulder.

'What is it?' she said, jerking herself free.

I laughed with relief. 'You gave me a fright.'

'Why?'

'Oh, never mind. How are you feeling?'

'Just two more days left,' she said, laughing mirthlessly, 'and this thing will be ripped from me.'

'It's not a thing,' I protested. 'It's a baby.'

'You don't understand, do you?' she asked agitatedly.

'All right, all right,' I soothed.

But she pushed me aside, leaped off the bed and fled out of the house.

I hurried after her.

She ran past the store, crossed the driveway and turned on to the road. I followed close behind her.

The moon was full, just as it had been that night, and she fled across the veld, stumbling over rocks and lurching into thorn bushes which gouged our arms and legs.

'Yasmin, come back!' I called, but she kept on running.

We were heading in the opposite direction from the village. Out of the shadows loomed the dark hump of a kopje. The veld was bathed in an eerie silence. I slowed down. 'Yasmin!' I shouted, but she merely waved me back. There were so many dangers ahead, large crevasses and dongas; worse still were the things that could not be seen in the dark. 'You'll get us both killed,' I called desperately.

'Go back!' she cried.

'No!' My voice was shrill with fear. 'You'll hurt yourself.'
She laughed.

I stopped to get my breath. We had reached the foot of the kopje and, thinking that I would go no further, Yasmin had slowed down too.

I was afraid, afraid of the dark and the veld. I wouldn't even go to the lavatory by myself at night. I thought of creatures out there – fearsome lizards called likkewaans, which grew to three or four feet, carnivores that preyed on the smaller, less ferocious but still ugly species. There were snakes like the boomslang, adders and deadly varieties of spiders – hairy monsters with a leg-span of at least four inches, scuttling around with devastating speed, small venomous button spiders and the grisly hunting spider.

I hoped that she'd turn back, for her sake, but more for mine. But she was moving again. I tucked my dress, which was hampering my progress, into my panties and began to climb after her, scrambling on all fours.

I caught up with her. Threw myself at her and knocked her off balance. We fell together, limbs intertwined. She fought me off, but fear had given me that extra strength.

She pushed and heaved in an attempt to break my hold. Desperation had given her strength too; my grip loosened but she was tiring. I pinned her down and she went limp. She opened her eyes and took a deep shuddering breath. 'It's all right, Meena.'

I hesitated.

'I'm all right now. I won't try anything stupid again,' she promised.

We studied each other for a moment.

'My goodness, you look a sight,' she laughed weakly, levering herself up off the ground.

Panting heavily, I managed a smile and helped her up. Then, supporting each other, we carefully picked our way past the thorn bushes and over the rocks to the cottage.

Thirty-One

In Aliwal North the doctor confirmed what we had already known: the foetus was fourteen weeks old. Although he was sympathetic, we told him nothing, because of our fear for a system of justice which punished the victim and not the offender.

Then we went to see the midwife. When we told her that Yasmin was fourteen weeks, she would have nothing to do with the abortion. Ma was devastated, but the midwife sympathetically explained the risks to Yasmin's life. Ma eventually accepted it, saying that it was God's will.

We spent the night with Nana's friend Queenie and returned home the following morning with Yasmin stretched out on the back seat looking deathly pale.

I was perched on the edge of the seat beside my sister, leaning over to the front between Ma and Nana. From time to time I turned my head to glance at Yasmin. I watched the movements of her eyes and knew that she was awake. The drive home was interminable, the road stretching ahead of us in an endless ribbon.

The grey dawn gave way to patches of orange as the sun crept over the horizon. I was touched by a strange longing, a vague nostalgia, that tugged at my insides. Nana sighed, wrapped up in her own thoughts and memories of other sunrises. Chin resting on the seat, I conjured up images of a sunrise, a lake and Yusuf . . .

We passed farmhouses where animals grazed in open kraals, then again we returned to miles of veld, scorched and baked by the sun.

The road fell away behind us. The DeSoto laboured up Penhoek; wisps of mist hovered and then trailed away. Down below the valley opened in a patchwork of brown and ecru while the hovering mist thinned and disintegrated.

The haze from cook-fires and braziers covered the valley like a ceiling splashed with the orange of the early morning sun.

Ma coasted down the hill passing the turn off to 'Twee Jonge Gezellen'. I felt my stomach knotting. An angry vein pulsed in Ma's temple. Afraid of upsetting Yasmin, we said nothing; instead, Ma pushed the car into gear before it could grind to a halt. The engine jerked to life.

When we passed the turn off to Sterkstroom she slowed down from force of habit, remembered that we were no longer there and sped by.

Nana shook her head. 'What are we going to do now?' she asked.

'I don't know, Mum.'

'If only she had spoken up earlier,' Nana said wearily.

We all suffered from that weariness which seemed to weigh down one's soul as it drowned in misery.

'Dora Oliphant died when she used a knitting needle to bring her baby down.' Although they spoke in low tones because they didn't want us to overhear, details surrounding Dora's death were common knowledge to any student who had ever attended SAPS.

When Nana said this, Ma shot an anxious glance over her shoulder to make sure that Yasmin had not heard. Yasmin's eyes were still closed.

'I don't know, Delia. I don't know.' Nana shuddered, a cold chill gripping her. 'I never had much call for the way the child was spoiled by you and Abdul. In my book, pretty isn't everything. I believed there was hope for her yet, because somewhere beneath all her vain and self-centred ways there was a spark of something, something that I couldn't quite put my finger on. She's always been deep. You never quite know what she's thinking even when she's hankering for something beyond her reach.' Nana shook her head. 'Because of all her fancy ideas I feared for her. Lord, how I feared for her.' She shook her head again. 'I hoped that she would accomplish something special with her life. That's why I thought private school was such a good idea. Perhaps I was wrong.' Nana sighed. 'Deep down I knew that some day she'd get into trouble but, Dear Lord, I never expected anything like this. It's too much. It really is too much.'

The tears slid down Ma's cheeks, but she quickly brushed them away.

We reached the turn off at McBain. Aware of the change in the road surface, Yasmin's lids flickered open. I watched her. 'Are you all right?' I asked.

Yasmin smiled bravely. It was an effort. She grimaced as the car bumped over a pothole.

Dust filled my nostrils. In the car it hung in little puffs. Ma tried to avoid the ruts in the driveway. But we were home and her shoulders automatically relaxed.

It was still early and the place was deathly still. For the first time I felt overpowered, like being crunched in the middle of a closing fist.

In the weeks that followed, Yasmin lost interest in everything. Ma had to persuade her to get out of bed long enough to bathe. Her beautiful hair was plastered to her scalp in limp strands. I waited anxiously for the old Yasmin to reappear while the two older women exchanged agonised glances above my head.

Thirty-Two

One afternoon, no longer able to cope with the tension at home, I slipped away and followed the railway line until I reached the crossing where so many people had been killed. I skipped over the lines and hurried towards the kopje. I wanted to get away, to sit on top of the world so that I could put things in perspective.

From the summit I could see McBain and the village. Alone in this vast open veld I nervously glanced over my shoulder to make sure that I wasn't caught unawares like Yasmin.

A cold breeze whipped at my hair and I huddled into my jacket. I turned to glance at the view stretching into the distance behind me. The dark railway tracks snaked out of sight. I remembered the night Yasmin and I had struggled here.

I climbed higher and found a flat boulder. I hoisted myself up. Down below, the thorn bushes were clustered in small clumps. The bright, orange-tipped aloe bush, erect, tall cacti with lance-like leaves crowned by racemes of bright orange flowers, stood aloof and majestic against the barren landscape.

I wondered if things would ever be the same again. Yasmin had always dominated our lives. Suddenly I felt a rush of resentment. It was always Yasmin this and Yasmin that. What was it about my sister that could make one love her passionately one moment and hate her the next?

Nana said that Yasmin attracted trouble like a magnet, but she had also said that this was a period of darkness. It was true that Yasmin couldn't be blamed for what had happened to her. I felt a twinge of guilt about the direction my thoughts had taken. I tried to banish them from my mind, but I couldn't. There would be another life. A child. Her child, who would end up disowned in its father's world and despised in its mother's world. I imagined a little face, tiny hands groping. I sat there for a long time trying to sort out my jumbled thoughts.

Startled, I realised that it was late. The sun had edged towards the horizon. Little rays of light fought to remain above the mountain, penetrating the clouds, bathing them in an incandescent light, but they were soon dragged down, leaving large shadows in their wake. I started to run, terrified that these shadows might catch up with me.

Nana and Ma decided to risk the scandal that would issue from a visit to a doctor in Queenstown, where we were known, rather than travel the distance to Aliwal North each time Yasmin needed a check-up.

'It's no one's business,' Nana said, hands on hips, ready for any confrontation. 'The only thing we have to worry about is Yasmin.'

Ma made the appointment to see Dr Hoffman.

In Queenstown I waited with Ma in the office while Dr Hoffman completed his examination of Yasmin.

He followed Yasmin out of the cubicle into his office, shutting the door.

'You have neglected your health. Look at all this,' he said, pointing to the reports on his desk. 'One thing after another. Are you a little bit crazy?'

Ma leaned over to catch a glimpse of these reports while Yasmin coloured, eyes blazing rebelliously.

'All right, never mind. I don't care about your craziness,' he said. 'I care about your baby.'

Yasmin glanced at the painting behind him. The scene was titled 'Platteland' and depicted an old farmhouse in the midst of wheat fields in the Orange Free State.

'Your pelvis is too small and your baby is in the breech position.'

Yasmin's eyes flickered.

'You have gained too much weight. There is no excuse for such neglect.' His glance reproached her.

Yasmin remained indifferent, obviously still uncaring about the baby. She had hoped right from the beginning that it would die. She had even thought of going the way of Dora Oliphant, but I told her that it would be a horrible way to end her life.

Dr Hoffman's lips were moving, but she didn't seem to hear him. She had that glazed look in her eyes.

Suddenly she winced, placing her hand against her stomach to ease the discomfort. She emerged from her dream-state.

'Was that the first time you have felt it move?'

138

She nodded.

He exchanged glances with Ma, who had remained silent all this time. 'Ja. It is a bit early, but not unusual.' Dr Hoffman studied her, his thick brows coming together. 'I want to see you next week again.'

Yasmin nodded, but the doctor noticed her lack of enthusiasm.

'What is wrong?' he demanded.

'Nothing,' Yasmin said tersely.

'All right, so be seeing you next week Monday. Okay?' He held the door open for us.

Ma smiled grimly. I could see that she was worried.

Thirty-Three

Papa's shoulders were stooped as though he were carrying some invisible burden. His whole posture was that of a man grown weary of life.

'I hope his heart doesn't act up again,' Ma said, watching him.

Yasmin grew bigger and more awkward, caring nothing about her health. She ate to excess against the doctor's instructions. She had gained fifty pounds and was enormous, able only to waddle around. Once she had accepted that nothing could be done to terminate the pregnancy, she bore it like a Stoic.

'I think she's going to have a girl,' Nana predicted. But Yasmin shut her ears and her mind. She had withdrawn from all of us, sitting by the stove like a statue through that cold winter while the rest of us worried about her.

Life went on in the rhythmic, endless cycle: in the spring the rains came, succouring the thirsty grass roots, washing away the dust which for months had crept over everything. The farmers wept for joy as the rains filled the rivers and gullies, the parched earth drinking up the moisture, healing the cracks and restoring the vitality to the land.

'Come on. Let's go for a walk,' I suggested one Sunday morning after the sky had cleared. The sun had come out and it was a beautiful, fresh day. 'The doctor says you need lots of exercise.'

Yasmin nodded listlessly. She had no interest at all in doing anything. I could understand, because she was so bloated that she must've been extremely uncomfortable. Through all this, she never once uttered a word of complaint though.

After the rain the veld was a festival of insect industry, life having returned to the slaked earth: butterflies, ants, termites, centipedes and slugs all scrambled for food.

I took huge gulps of air while, above the pale green stubble, thousands of white butterflies hovered and lurched. The air was alive with the flutter of wings.

'Yasmin,' I said timidly. 'I'm so sorry about everything. Talk to me, please.'

She stopped in her tracks and gave me a long searching glance. 'I know that you're sorry. I am too. Perhaps some day I'll talk about this, but not now. Maybe some day I'll be able to make all of this up to you.'

'What do you mean? This isn't your fault. You have nothing to be ashamed of.'

'Well, maybe . . . But I have done some thinking and I know that I have to do something with my life. I have to make a decision. You know it's not my nature to dwell on the past, but if I had a chance to live my life over again, there are a few things that I'd do differently.'

'Like what, Yasmin?'

Yasmin glanced into the distance. 'You know . . .'

'Tell me.'

'Don't be silly. I can't tell you everything.'

'What are you going to do when the baby's born?' I asked.

Yasmin abruptly turned away. She had shut the door again. 'I don't want to talk about it.'

'It's only a baby, Yas. The poor thing knows nothing about you, or its father, or the way in which it came to life.'

'I told you I don't want to talk about it,' Yasmin snapped.

'It's innocent.'

'No it's not. It breathes. It moves. It knows everything. How could it be innocent?'

I felt the blood drain from my face. Apparently my sister was not going to listen to reason.

'Let's go back home,' Yasmin said abruptly, turning back. 'I'm not in the mood for any of this.'

Thirty-Four

We were sitting outside on the verandah one night when Yasmin went into labour. She had been very quiet all evening and when she drew a sharp breath we knew immediately. The spasm took her breath away and she looked up, eyes filled with fear.

Ma phoned the hospital in Queenstown. Then she quickly got Yasmin into the car with the rest of the family piling in. She was concerned because Yasmin wasn't due for another three weeks yet. Papa sat in the front seat, staring into the darkness, occasionally muttering and massaging his head, as he did whenever he was troubled.

Nana and I sat in the back seat, comforting Yasmin each time she cried out. Papa never turned his head, but he seemed to cringe, sinking deeper into the seat each time she had a contraction.

Dr Hoffman was angry because we had not come sooner. Ma tried to explain that we had left the moment Yasmin's contractions had started.

He swore softly in German and rushed down the hallway. Yasmin's eyes flickered; she was aware of movements and sounds. There seemed to be a strange, ethereal quality to this scene.

She was tossed on to a stretcher and rushed to the labour-room. Dr Hoffman's voice reached us through the door, shouting for her to bear down. As soon as the nurses were out sight, Ma and I peeped through the small window. Her legs were up in a stirrup and one of the nurses had the syringe ready.

I recognised the sickly, sweet odour of ether. Soon it would be surging through her veins, freezing her blood.

Yasmin was terrified and cried out for Ma. Ma grasped my hand with such force that I winced. She was facing away from us and we could only see the top of her head and her stirruped legs.

One of the nurses saw us and shouted us away from the door, but

142

the moment she was out of sight we were back there again.

Yasmin writhed and struggled, pushing until her body, arched and rigid, lifted off the bed.

The young nurse leaning over her gave her encouragement. 'You'll be all right,' she urged, but I wondered if the words had got through to Yasmin, who by this time was drifting on a cloud of narcosis.

She lifted her head. Dr Hoffman was squatting out of sight, peering between her raised legs. Only his voice could be heard.

'I can see the head,' he called gruffly. 'Bear down now!'

Yasmin did not respond.

'Come on! Dammit!' Dr Hoffman's angry voice sent a chill through us. 'Do you want to kill the baby?'

'Yes! Yes! I want to kill it!' she screamed.

'You are mad. Get the tray!' he shouted at the nurse. 'The baby is in the passage!'

We heard the clatter of stainless steel on stainless steel and my mind numbed with terror for my sister.

'What are you doing to me?' Yasmin cried.

'Come on, push!' Dr Hoffman shouted.

'Leave me alone!' Yasmin begged.

'Here, let me help.' Dr Hoffman had appeared from below somewhere. It had to be from hell, because at that moment he was like a demon. The nurses moved aside while he placed her right foot against his shoulder.

'You hate me!' he shouted. 'You have your chance to fight me now. Come on.'

In a surge of helpless rage she kicked against him.

'Good! Good!' he cried.

They placed a mask over her face. Dr Hoffman disappeared below again and when he straightened up we saw it! The tiniest speck of humanity, covered in blood and birth-fluid, eyes tightly shut, writhing in the doctor's hands. Ma and I rushed to tell the others. We heard the cry; it was weak but persistent.

Thirty-Five

The baby was a beautiful little girl with light grey eyes and golden hair. She was the most beautiful infant I had ever seen. My heart went out to the tiny morsel so obviously despised by its mother. None of us could tear ourselves away from the nursery, where the baby remained in an incubator because it was so small.

'Yasmin, you can't take your anger out on the child. It's not her fault,' Ma pleaded.

But Yasmin merely turned her head towards the wall.

'What are we going to do, Abdul?' Ma asked.

'We're going to take our grandchild home when she's well, whether Yasmin wants it or not.' Papa said.

'Yasmin, you'll have to name the baby.'

'Do what you want,' she said listlessly.

'Why don't you call her Fatima?' Papa suggested.

'Fine. We'll call her Fatima,' she said, shrugging her shoulders disinterestedly. She hadn't even seen the baby yet.

Nana and Ma exchanged glances.

Yasmin was discharged a week later and two weeks later the baby was strong enough to come home. Yasmin remained detached from both the baby and the family, displaying very little interest in either. The three of us doted on Fatima, tending to her every need.

'You've got to pull yourself together, Yasmin. Your baby needs you,' Ma reproached her over and over again, but Yasmin was in such a deep depression that none of us could reach her, not even Dr Hoffman, who had tried. Ma had been obliged to tell him parts of the story.

Dr Hoffman had been appalled that none of us had reported the incident right away. 'If you had taken her to a doctor right away, things might have been different. Now, you can prove nothing.'

'It would have been a waste of time. He's white,' Ma said bitterly.

144

When the doctor heard this, he shook his head and lowered his eyes. What could he say, I wondered.

For two months we struggled to get through to Yasmin. Then quite unexpectedly she seemed to recover and was jaunty again, spending hours before the mirror, curling her hair and applying her make-up. Ma watched, filled with misgivings. Nana too stole long penetrating glances at her.

'What are you doing?' Nana demanded.

'I'm making myself presentable,' Yasmin responded. 'Isn't that what you want?'

'It's what you want that counts,' Ma interjected.

'Oh no. Up to now it's been what you want.' Yasmin got up from the dresser, her eyes blazing with defiance. 'I had that baby because you wanted it.'

'What are you talking about, child? You know that it was too late. There was nothing we could do.'

'I hate it! I never want to see it!' she said, storming out of the room.

'Yasmin!' Ma was appalled. She looked at Nana with a sense of helplessness. Nana shook her head.

Ma's face was gaunt with distress. There were new undertones to Yasmin's emotional state. Nana too sensed it and was afraid.

'Don't try to bottle your feelings up. Talk about it. You'll feel a lot better,' I urged. She was in the kitchen reluctantly helping me to prepare Fatima's formula. 'Life isn't all that bad. You have your baby now and . . .'

'Life! What do you know about life!' Yasmin cried, clenching my arm.

I stared at her in astonishment.

'What do you know about life?' she demanded, her voice hoarse with emotion.

'What do you mean?'

'I mean like living and hurting. Not hiding out.'

Cautiously I moistened my lips. Of course I know a little bit, I thought. I'd also been hurting for a long time. 'I know,' I said, trying to free myself from her frenzied hold. But she wouldn't let go.

'What do you know?' Yasmin demanded, face contorted. 'Do you know about birth . . . and . . . and wanting to die?'

'Yes,' I croaked.

145

'How can you know?' she said. 'All your life you've been protected by two fussing women. In their eyes you're a saint. You can't do a thing wrong, can you? I'm the devil. Maybe I am. I've been through it all.' She paused for breath. 'I wanted to tear that baby out bit by bit. How can I be expected to love it after all the loathing and hate I feel for its father?'

'Then hate the father, but not the child!'

'I've had nine months for all this hate to ferment!' The words were torn from her and she gasped, each word like the thrust of a knife.

'What makes you think you're an authority on pain and suffering? What about the suffering of others? What about that baby?' I demanded.

Yasmin covered her ears.

'Yes, your baby?' I cried. 'How can you blame a helpless little baby? And what about us? We have to stand by and see you tearing yourself apart, watching while you turn from that child which is a part of you. Don't you think we suffer too?'

Yasmin hunched her shoulders, pressing her hands against her ears.

'Instead of pulling yourself together . . . pulling your life together, you're wallowing in self-pity. You still think you're so damn special! Sometimes I think you deserve to be miserable.'

Yasmin withdrew her hands. 'I don't think I'm so special.' Her voice had lost its brittleness.

I screwed the top on to the feeder. Suddenly I felt worn out.

'Forget everything I said.' Her voice had changed again. It flowed pure and sweet, like syrup, chilling me to the bone.

146

Thirty-Six

That night, unable to sleep, I crept out of the bedroom and went to lie in the sitting-room. I stretched out on the settee and squeezed my eyes shut until bright points of light shimmered and danced before my aching eyeballs. I tried to force myself out of this miserable environment into the tranquil world of my childhood, but it seemed impossible to make that transition.

The little space in which I had taken refuge as a child no longer existed. Instead, I felt myself being forced into a tunnel which stretched beyond the darkness of my immediate surroundings.

A fine film of moisture formed on my body. Although my hands were clammy with fear, I soared forward, heart pounding anxiously. I wanted to enter that tunnel, but fear held me back.

Suddenly a voice called. The urgency of the tone dragged me back. I kept my eyes shut, part of me not wanting to relinquish this dream.

'Meena! Meena!'

It was Yasmin.

Reluctantly I opened my eyes. My vision slowly adjusted to the darkness until I was able to discern the faint outline of my sister's body, her nightgown tightly wrapped about her.

'I know you're here. I can hear you breathing,' Yasmin whispered.

'I'm on the settee.'

The disembodied figure in the white nightgown drifted towards me. I watched with a sense of macabre fascination as my sister's face finally became visible in the light from the window.

Yasmin stopped by the settee, groping in the darkness. Her hand brushed against my legs and I quickly withdrew from her touch.

'Move up, Meena,' she hissed impatiently.

I could see her clearly now.

'I want to talk to you, Meena.'

'What about?'

'About the baby . . . I'm going away. I can't bear to cause any of you any more unhappiness.'

I laughed mirthlessly. 'You're going to leave your baby and you want my approval?'

'I can't keep that child. I've tried . . . I can't,' her voice was ragged and tormented. She took several deep breaths to keep herself from crying. 'I'm sorry.'

'Have you mentioned this to Ma and Nana?'

I sensed her shaking her head in the darkness. I pulled myself up. 'You've always known how to hurt people. You're an expert at that, especially hurting those who love you. And after you've shattered them, you turn around, flutter your eyelashes and say you're sorry. When are you going to grow up? When are you going to face your responsibilities? Face the fact that Fatima is your daughter, and nothing you do is going to change that!' The anger flew off me like sparks off a flint.

'None of this was my fault . . .' Yasmin protested.

'It's never your fault,' I mocked. 'It's always the next person. You never cease to amaze me. Do you know what your attitude is doing to this family?'

Yasmin remained silent.

'No, you'll never know,' I said, her silence reaching me. 'You don't care about anything or anyone.'

'I'm sorry,' Yasmin whispered.

'Sorry won't help any more,' I cried. 'It doesn't bring the broken pieces together.'

Yasmin remained silent. I flicked the light on beside the settee. Her eyes were tightly shut against the pain of my words. She sensed the light and they flew open, lashes fluttering frantically like those of a trapped bird.

I stared at her, brought my face up close to hers and in a voice of a stranger hissed, 'I should never have pulled you back off that kopje.'

Yasmin dropped her glance; she had never seen me so bitter before.

'Maybe we would all have been better off with you dead,' I said harshly.

Crushed by my words, the colour drained from her face and she lowered her glance. Seeing her so devastated, I felt dreadful about my outburst. I went to her and put my arms about her neck; her

148

head sank on to my shoulder and I held her close, sharing in her anguish as only a sister could.

Yasmin was subdued. I didn't know whether to tell Ma about her plans to leave or not, because there was a new note of hostility between them. They weren't speaking, avoiding each other for days on end. It was all building up to something big. That much was obvious. I hoped though that Yasmin would eventually change her mind about her baby.

The storm broke one Thursday night when Yasmin, in a fit of depression, neglected to feed Fatima.

'Starving your own child! You're a monster!' Ma cried. 'A devil!' she shouted in anger. Without a word, Yasmin turned and walked away.

'Come back here and take care of your baby!'

Yasmin ignored her.

'You get back.' Ma, blinded by rage, caught hold of her and swung her around. Then she struck her with such force that Yasmin was thrown off balance.

It was the first time in Yasmin's life that either of our parents had ever raised a hand at her. She was stunned, but the look she gave Ma was filled with such unspeakable contempt that Ma, startled, took a step back.

That night the house was very silent. Something deep and disturbing had happened and we all sensed it.

Then on Friday morning, when we got up, Yasmin was gone. Ma sat staring at the fire, the baby in her arms. Papa went to her. He knelt down unsteadily, but she remained motionless. He put his arm about her shoulder; still she did not move. Finally, she got up, handed the baby to me and went to the phone. She spoke to the police in Queenstown, phoned Baboo in Jo'burg and spoke to Aishabhen. She asked them to let us know if any of them or their friends heard from Yasmin.

'Where does one begin to look?' Ma asked.

She drove around in a daze, conducting a senseless search. Then she ranted about Yasmin's selfishness. 'What about her child. Does she not care?'

Nana shook her head.

'She's always thought only of herself, never considered the next person,' Ma cried.

'It's too late to think about that now,' Nana said.

149

Ma broke down and cried then, her body heaving as she sobbed uncontrollably.

There was nothing that could comfort her. She cried for hours, all the pent-up frustrations, disappointments and anger released in a torrent of tears.

'It's a period of darkness,' Nana explained. 'It comes into everyone's life. Yasmin chose her own course a long time ago.'

Ma tried to compose herself. She wanted to generate an aura of calm strength, but Nana was the one we leaned on in those difficult days.

The house seemed desolate.

'Yasmin is strong-willed,' Nana said. 'She's a survivor.'

Ma desperately needed reassurance and Nana gave it gladly.

'Yasmin's more capable of surviving out there than any one else I know,' Nana said. 'The baby will be better off with us and she knows it. I think she did this for the child's sake.'

I tried to blot out Yasmin but, as always, she was dominating our lives, even in her absence.

'There was nothing here for Yasmin,' Nana remarked. 'This place is like a desert.'

'I thought that together we could provide a small oasis of happiness,' Ma remarked, eyes brimming.

Nana shook her head. 'Not here, not in this country. It won't be long before they'll be back again with their dogs and their guns.'